ALL ABOUT CHINCHILLAS

KAREN ZEINERT

To Scott and Brad

(t.f.h.)

Contents

Acknowledgments

This book would not have been possible without the help and support of some very special people.

I want to acknowledge and thank Reginald Chapman, M. F. Chapman's son, for sharing family photos and providing information about his father's early chinchilla adventures; Fred and Mary Lou Krueger for providing mutations for pictures; Cecil and Yvonne Featherston for providing props for both photos and a writer's wavering confidence; and my husband, who spent many hours photographing animals that didn't want to sit still.

"Thank you's" are in order, too, to all of the "old-timers," the chin ranchers who learned by doing and shared their accumulated knowledge so willingly at shows, in seminars, and in trade publications.

Introduction

Chinchillas are easy animals to like, and when my husband and I became ranchers about 14 years ago, we treated the animals more as pets than pelt producers. We named each one, marveled at how cute they were, played with them, and spoiled them with treats.

Once in awhile we received requests for pets, and at first it was honestly hard for us to think of those expensive animals in that way even though we were hardly treating our herd in a businesslike manner. The fact that so little written information was available for potential pet owners made us leery about selling animals that needed to be raised via specific guidelines. The crash course we gave on diet and housing while the new owner cuddled a bundle of fur failed to make us feel any better.

As more chinchillas were sold by us and other ranchers and people began to buy pairs so they could raise kits, I felt it was time to put something on paper, something a pet owner could come back to again and again as the need for information arose.

Gathering that information was difficult. No two owners seem to do everything exactly the same way.

Therefore, the advice on the following pages is really a composite of what has worked for our animals and what is recommended by most chinchilla owners. If you are a chin owner, I hope the information that follows will help your pet thrive. If you are not a chin owner, I hope the contents will encourage you to become more familiar with a unique and interesting animal.

A Chinchilla
is . . .

With so many chinchillas living on ranches, in pet stores, and in zoos, it seems strange that most people lack familiarity with the animal. Yet owners who are often asked to describe a chin find they must resort to using well-known animals to help an inquirer picture one. Usually the animal is described as a chubby squirrel with big ears or as a small rabbit with short ears and a long tail. While both descriptions help one to visualize a chin, albeit roughly, neither really helps someone understand just what is a chinchilla.

A chinchilla is a rodent. It is classified as a member of the order Rodentia, a group of animals named from the Latin word *rodere*, which literally means "to gnaw." It's the teeth that do the gnawing that set rodents apart from other mammals. Rodents have two incisors in the upper jaw, no canines (the eye teeth normally located next to the incisors), and a varying number of back or cheek (molar) teeth. The space between the incisors and cheek teeth is called the "diastema." When a rodent gnaws away, it can pull its lips into the diastema to keep chips and debris from entering its mouth.

While rodents share common dental patterns, three different skull structures allow scientists to break the order down and classify rodents into three suborders. **Sciuromorphs** (squirrels, beavers, and gophers) have a jaw muscle attached to each cheek-bone as do most mammals. **Myomorphs** (mice, hamsters, and rats) have jaw muscles that pass through two small openings—one on each side of the skull—to an anchorage at each side of the nose. **Hystricomorphs** (porcupines, guinea pigs, and chins) have massive cheek-bones and two large openings in the skull that allow jaw muscles to pass straight up from the jaw to the sides of the face.

Each of the three suborders is broken down into families, and one of the hystricomorph families is the Chinchillidae. It includes four species of viscacha, the chinchilla's closest relatives, and two species of chins.

Viscachas (genera *Lagidium*, the three species of mountain viscachas, and genus *Lagostomus*, with one species of mountain viscacha) are similar to chins in appearance except that they have black and white horizontal stripes on their faces. Like chins, viscachas are South American natives, nocturnal animals, vegetarians, and inhabitants of burrows or crevices located in high altitudes.

The two species of chins, *Chinchilla brevicaudata* and *C. lanigera* (sometimes listed as *C. laniger* or *C. lanigar*, incorrectly) differ in appearance. Both species have long hindlimbs, short forelimbs, four toes, and flexible fingers, but *C. brevicaudata* has a thick neck and shoulders and is heavily furred with coarse hair that is light gray in color and often tinged with a yellowish cast. Its ears are shorter than those of *C. lanigera*, and its nose is flatter, giving the animal a stocky appearance. *C. lanigera* individuals are narrow in the neck and shoulders—ranchers use the term "dipped-neck" when describing them—and lightly furred. Moreover, the fur is very silky and usually medium to dark gray, with a bright bluish cast. Their faces are usually pointed and the ears elongated, making them appear very long and lean.

C. brevicaudata is now extinct in most of its original range, from the high Andes of Bolivia and Peru to northern Chile and Argentina. Some C. lanigera still live in northern Chile, but the species is practically extinct in the wild. Both are protected by their governments, and wild populations are on the U.S. Endangered Species list. Hunting or trapping them is forbidden.

Both species were brought into the United States for breeding purposes. It was hoped that the two could be bred together to produce offspring that were large, blocky, and covered with silky fur. Early attempts to cross the two reportedly resulted in sterility in the male offspring, and, since the C. lanigera individuals produced the best fur, the other species was dropped from most breeding programs. Therefore it is generally assumed that most of the animals in the United States are descendants of the species C. lanigera.

However, since two very distinct types of animals appear on ranches today—one that breeders call a "brevicaudata type" and another referred to as a "costina type" (often incorrectly labeled as another species; it's a type of C. lanigera)—one could argue that today's light gray, large, blocky, heavily furred animals have enough characteristics to classify them as the real C. brevicaudata, not just "brevicaudata types." On the other hand, others argue that so many animals have been bred by people who have experimented with developing mutations and different strains that the genetic pool, which is vast and mixed, may have produced a variety of

The first chinchilla unit in North America, photographed in Los Angeles in 1925. Photo through the courtesy of Reginald Chapman.

types, all of *C. lanigera.* Mammalogists—scientists who study mammals—consider all domesticated chins to be a single species, *C. lanigera.*

It is certain that once chins were captured, caged, and bred for fur production, dramatic changes took place in their appearance, as anyone who has ever seen a mounted wild chinchilla in a natural history museum can attest. Those changes were the result of a big gamble taken by M. F. Chapman, the man who brought chinchillas to the United States.

Chapman's Chins

M. F. Chapman was working as a mining engineer for Anaconda Copper in Chile in 1918 when he saw his first chinchilla. A native who had captured one of the rodents had taken it to Chapman's camp to sell. Chapman bought the animal and, as he cared for his new pet, developed a real interest in it, one that would last the rest of his life. In fact, Chapman soon wanted more than one chinchilla; he began to dream about owning a whole herd!

The Californian certainly wasn't the first person to admire chinchillas. Natives cherished the animal's fur and had been making warm, lightweight garments from chinchilla pelts long before the first Spanish explorers arrived in South America in the 1500's. Once the explorers spotted the garments, they insisted on adding pelts to their cargoes for their return trips. They introduced chinchilla fur to Europe, where it quickly became known as the fur of princes and princesses when the limited number of pelts were used to trim royal robes and gowns.

An Englishman, Sir Richard Hawkins, also admired chinchillas. He described the rodent in the following terms in a book he wrote in 1593:

"They (South Americans) have little beastes like unto a squirrell, but that he is gray; his skinne is the most delicate, soft, and curious furre that I have seene. . . . They call this beast chinchilla, and of them they have great abundance."

Chapman wasn't the first one to dream about having a herd of them either. Several dreamers had captured chinchillas for breeding purposes but usually lost them while bringing them down from the mountains. One group did survive, though, and became the first inhabitants of the first chinchilla farm, near San Antonio de los Cobre, Argentina. But, although 36 animals survived the trip down the mountains, they didn't thrive in captivity, and the enterprise failed.

It's not clear whether or not Chapman knew about the farm in Argentina, but he did know about previous attempts to capture chinchillas when he decided to try to catch a herd himself.

About a year after he saw his first chin, Chapman applied to the Chilean government for permission to capture several and transport them to the United States to start North America's first herd. By this time, however, the animals were close to extinction as a result of excessive trapping for pelts, so the Chilean government was reluctant to grant trapping privileges, let alone give permission to take chinchillas out of the country. Persistence on Chapman's part paid off, though, and eventually the government relented on both issues.

A trapping party of 23 men was hired to capture as many chinchillas as possible, but chins were so scarce that it took the party three years to catch 11 good enough to breed.

Since the chinchilla's native habitat was approximately 12,000 feet above sea level where it was cool and dry, Chapman planned to give the animals time—lots of

M. F. Chapman, the man who brought the first chinchillas to America, and Pete, who often rode around on Chapman's shoulders while the rest of the herd was being fed and cared for. Photo through the courtesy of Reginald Chapman.

time—to acclimate themselves before boarding a ship for California. He believed that other trappers had failed to keep their charges alive because they expected them to adapt to new surroundings too quickly. Therefore, his chinchillas' cages were lowered down the mountains gradually during a 12-month period, cooled with blocks of ice when necessary, and shaded from direct sunlight. His careful handling of the animals paid off, and all 11 chins survived the trip down the mountains.

The animals required special conditions once aboard the ship, too. A constant supply of ice was needed to keep the cages cool, and the Chapmans—Mrs. Chapman had joined him on his endeavor—took turns stocking the ice compartments in the cages as well as draping cooling wet towels around them.

Shortly after crossing the Equator, the animals shed their fur; by the time they arrived in Los Angeles (February 21, 1923) cold was more of a threat to the herd's health than was heat. Even so, the hardy creatures had done more than just survive a long journey: they had multiplied. A kit was born aboard the ship.

Over the years Chapman experimented with both housing and diet. As the herd adjusted and thrived, livestock was finally offered for sale.

Since the chinchillas were quite expensive—$3200 a pair—the idea of keeping them as pets was more than a little out of the reach of most people, especially when the Depression came. Actually, most people purchasing chins at that time did so on a group basis, with members buying shares in a pair of animals, hoping to sell lots of livestock in the future.

By the middle 1960's, thousands of chins were being raised on ranches throughout the United States and Canada. As their numbers continued to increase, some animals were finally offered as pets. One advertiser in a

One of the concrete houses Chapman used to house chinchillas. Although the front door was padlocked to prevent theft, thieves managed to steal over a third of Chapman's herd in 1931. He was never able to recover the animals. Photo through the courtesy of Reginald Chapman.

Winter in chinchilla country. (M. F. Chapman on the left.)

national magazine offered pet chinchillas for sale for $100 each. The ad described them as "little fur balls—quiet, odorless, and vermin free"—and it should have included gentle and curious as well.

Chapman probably never intended that the animals should become pets, even though he certainly developed a real attachment to some of his breeders. Although most chins today are raised for pelt production, more and more are available as pets. That is a fortunate development, because with careful selection a healthy chinchilla can give years of pleasure to its owner.

Choosing a Chinchilla

Before selecting any chinchilla, a potential owner needs to examine a chinchilla's limitations. It can't be taken for a walk like a dog, at least not on a hot, sunny day. It can't have the run of the house like a cat. Once loose and unsupervised, it will sharpen its incisors on the furniture. Since it's most active at night, someone wanting an alert, playful pet in the afternoon would be disappointed in a chin.

Other animals (such as dogs) in the household may cause problems if a chin is added. Although a number of ranchers have dogs that enter their chinchilla units regularly, most are cautious about leaving one unattended with the chins even if they've never encountered difficulty between the animals. Actually, most dogs get along very well with chins; some have even been put to work in the chinchilla units locating and then gently prodding and pushing "escapees" into the open so the rancher can catch them easily. But, since it's hard to judge how any dog might react to a chin, you will have to be prepared to keep them apart or supervise them until you're sure the dog won't harm the chin.

Cats pose less of a threat to chinchillas than dogs do—one rancher raised 40 cats without incident while caring for his herd of chins—but here again, extra effort will be needed to supervise the animals initially. If you raise exotic pets like snakes or ferrets, you must be prepared to keep the animals separated; they are natural enemies.

One other factor to consider before buying a chin for a pet is the age of the pet handlers. If very young children are going to play with the animal, an adult should be prepared to be present. Chins like to nibble on things to see what they're like. A small child may interpret a light nip on the hand as a bite and become frightened.

In short, chins are different and not the pet for just anyone.

On the other hand, being different has advantages. Unlike dogs or cats, a chinchilla is strictly a vegetarian and therefore inexpensive and easy to feed. Pellets and hay, a chin's dietary staples, are readily available. A chinchilla does not need daily outings. If enough food and water are provided, a chin can be left alone in its cage for a day or two. Unlike other fur-bearing animals, a chin has no odor noticeable to humans and can be kept almost anywhere in the house or apartment without being offensive to even the most sensitive nose. Although it can cry and bark like many other animals, it seldom makes noises. Like puppies and kittens, it is an inquisitive, intelligent animal with an ability to create its own games and thus is fun to play with and to watch. But even though chinchillas are long-lived—they can live ten years or more—they never seem to outgrow the puppy-like fun stage. Because a chin is different, it often attracts lots of attention for both the pet and its owner.

BUYING YOUR CHINCHILLA

Where can a pet chinchilla be found? One of the best places to start looking is in a local pet store. Even though most pet shops will stock only one or two of the animals at best, and some never show them at all, most pet shop owners know where to find chinchillas; some are even able to fill special requests regarding age and color.

One might also contact a nearby chinchilla rancher. Locating one is not as easy as finding a pet store, but a check in the Yellow Pages of the local phone book or those of nearby cities kept in the public library might result in an address or two. Local feed mills often make or stock feed for chinchilla breeders and may be able to provide a would-be pet owner with a rancher's location.

Most ranchers have animals that would make good pets, but be forewarned that not every animal on the ranch is for sale. Many of them are worth hundreds of dollars, and some are almost priceless because of their special genetic make-up. Ranchers have been known to turn down $1000 offers for an animal. Anyway, pet owners can be consoled by the fact that one doesn't need a national grand show champion to have a fine pet. A gentle, healthy chinchilla will do just fine.

In order to judge both temperament and health, anyone wishing to buy a chinchilla should ask for permission to hold and examine an animal closely before buying it. Begin by approaching the cage slowly, speaking softly. Loud or "swishing" noises—the kind of sound nylon jackets make when the sleeves rub against the body of the jacket—terrify the animals. (Many ranchers believe the "swishing" noises make the chinchillas think snakes are present.) Sudden movements, especially those that produce shadows, are frightening, too, making it very difficult to catch and handle the animal, let alone evaluate its temperament.

After the door to the cage is opened, a chin should be given a few minutes to become acquainted with a new handler. Let it sniff and "nibble" (chins are a little like babies, putting everything in the mouth) at the hands that are going to hold it. While chins will chew on rings and watches and tug at cuffs or sleeves, very few will bite hard except in self-defense. "Nibbling" is also a way of showing affection in their world, and mates often chew on each other's ears, around the eyes, and under their chins.

The best way to catch a chinchilla is to reach around it on both sides as the animal faces its handler, grasping the tail firmly with one hand and supporting the animal with the other. It should *never* be grabbed by the fur. One of the defense mechanisms the animal has is its ability to release its fur if caught. Thus anyone trying to grab it by the fur will have a handful of hair and a half-naked animal.

A gentle animal—and a good potential pet—will not cry or struggle frantically to get away unless it has been unduly frightened. If scratched behind the ears or under the chin, it may relax even for a stranger. When put back into the cage, it will come to the door for more attention.

Another advantage in actually holding the animal is the opportunity it provides to evaluate the animal's physical condition. It is very hard to judge a chinchilla's health without holding it, since the fur may be an inch or so long, giving the impression of a much larger, sturdier animal than it actually is.

A chinchilla's type should be taken into account when judging its physical condition. A heavy *brevicaudata* type animal is not necessarily in better health than a long, thin *lanigera* type. If the animal being examined is fully grown (that is, over eight months old and weighing over 16 ounces) and it feels solid, the animal is probably healthy regardless of whether it's narrow or wide in the neck.

Look at the animal's eyes to be sure. They should be bright and shiny. Watery, weepy eyes are a warning of health problems in progress or about to come.

A horse's mouth is often checked before the animal is purchased. A chinchilla's mouth should be examined, too. It may be reluctant to show its "pearlies," but if offered a treat of sunflower seeds or raisins (or allowed to chew on a pencil for a minute or two) the animal will provide the opportunity for a quick look at the front teeth, which should be creamy yellow in color, never white. The top teeth should overlap the bottom ones, and both sets should be fairly straight across. Furthermore, the animal should finish the treat quickly, not paw at its mouth or drool. (Check for previous drooling under the chin. The chin should not be wet or matted.) Usually a chinchilla will beg for more before it has swallowed the treat in its mouth. Tooth problems are a serious threat to a chinchilla's well-being, and animals with such problems should be avoided by pet owners.

There is no ideal age at which to purchase a chinchilla. Most babies are weaned at six to eight weeks of age, and it's probably best to leave the weaner in the shop or on the ranch for at least a week or two after that. Weaning is stressful, and being taken from a mother and placed in new surroundings with a new owner may be too stressful for a young chin, leading to illness or even death. Most people like to purchase a young animal about three or four months old, but an older one can make a pleasant pet, too.

It matters little whether the potential pet is male or female, since neither sex is notably calmer, more attractive, or more likable. Each animal has its own personality, and it's the animal's personality that should be of paramount consideration when deciding which one to buy.

While most pet owners prefer to begin their chinchilla-owning experiences with the purchase of a single animal, there's nothing wrong with buying a pair—one male, one female—as long as the owner is prepared for the care of potential offspring. A word of caution, though. The pair should already be living together when purchased. If two unacquainted animals are brought home, they must be paired gradually. Two males or two females cannot be housed together. **Never! No exceptions!**

CHINCHILLA COLORS

Most pet owners have a gray, known among ranchers as "standard," chinchilla. It is the original and most prevalent color, with variations in shading ranging from pale gray to almost black.

However, chinchillas are available in other colors besides gray, and some are sold as pets. Common mutant colors include white, beige, and black.

Chinchilla mutations appeared on ranches as early as the 1940's, but the first really important mutant, a white male, didn't arrive until 1955. Born on a ranch in North Carolina, Whitie was a prolific breeder and the beginning of the line known as Wilson Whites. Unlike true albinos, which have pink ears and reddish pink eyes, Whitie's descendants have black-tipped ears and black eyes. A mosaic, the occasional result of breeding a Wilson White to a standard, is a white animal with patches of gray or silver. Mosaics, which were common among mutation ranchers about ten years ago, are hard to find today. No two are ever exactly alike.

Another important mutation, a beige female, was born September 29, 1955, on the Oregon ranch of Ned Jensen. Jensen was not interested in working with the animal. Instead, he showed it to a number of ranchers, hoping to find someone who would be willing to invest the necessary time and effort to see whether the mutation could be reproduced. Although most ranchers considered it a "freak," unable to reproduce its color (or worse yet, sterile), Nick Tower, a nearby rancher, decided to buy the animal.

Tower faced an enormous challenge in working with the little, thin, weak, and listless female. Upon close examination, he discovered that the beige had serious dental problems and therefore only a limited amount of time left. Although clipping and shaping her front teeth made it easier for her to eat, her cheek teeth were overly sensitive, making the consumption of typical chinchilla feed almost impossible. Tower modified her diet and continued to reshape her teeth the best he could; he thereby helped her achieve enough strength and vitality to breed. Six months after he purchased her, she was paired with a standard male. Four months later she delivered a healthy beige male. The young beige grew up to become an outstanding breeder. As livestock was sold to other ranchers, beige mutations—known as "Crown of Sunset Beiges"—became an important part of the chinchilla industry.

In 1956, Bob Gunning, a rancher in the state of Washington, purchased a standard animal known as "Dirty Face" because of the unusually dark markings around her eyes and mouth. Mr. Gunning, through selective breeding, was able to extend the dark patches of coloring on the face all the way down the grotzen (the center back strip of a fur pelt), producing another mutation known as a black velvet, or the Gunning Black.

Over the years other mutations such as sapphires and charcoals appeared on ranches. When these mutations were bred to each other, variations in coloring began to appear, including whites with sprinkles of beige hair mixed in and beiges with dark velvety fur.

One of the newest mutations to be raised in the United States is called the Sullivan Violet, an animal with a clear white belly and a lavender (some call it a pinkish violet) grotzen. The first violets were born on a ranch in Rhodesia (today Zimbabwe), Africa, sometime in the mid-1960's. The herd was put up for sale when the owner decided to flee Rhodesia's civil war. The chins were first moved to Johannesburg, South Africa, and later flown to California. The herd is presently housed on the Loyd Sullivan ranch in California. At this writing, Sullivan Violets are available in very limited numbers for breeding stock. They are far too expensive and valuable genetically to be sold as pets yet. Mutation ranchers are anxiously watching the violet's progress. Some believe it may be the chinchilla color of the future.

Whether you purchase a standard, beige, white, black, or any other color of chinchilla, a word of advice is in order. Animals sold as pets are meant to be just that, pets. They are not meant to be bred for fur production. Even if the pet is the prettiest animal on the block, it may not have the genetic material to produce top quality pelts or breeding livestock, the only kind desired in the fur business. One cannot have a pet today and a pelt producer tomorrow. (But that's not to say that a pet owner can't raise more pets.)

One final caution before heading home with that incredibly soft ball of fur: take along about a two-week

Tiers of chinchilla cages in a commercial chinchilla ranch. Photo by John A. Zeinert.

supply of whatever feed the animal has been eating. A chin's diet may be changed, but the change must be made gradually.

Feeding Chinchillas

In the wild, chinchillas ate seeds, grasses, and yareta, a large woody-rooted plant (family Umbelliferae, genus *Laretia*) that South American natives gathered for fuel. Mr. Chapman used local vegetation to feed his herd while he brought it down from the mountains, but once the herd arrived in Los Angeles significant dietary changes had to be made.

Chapman tried to duplicate his herd's natural diet as much as possible, so his chins ate hay, fresh greens, bark from fruit trees (to replace yareta), and a variety of grains. At first the animals experienced great difficulty adjusting to their new feed. Some died, and those that lived did not thrive. As Chapman continued to test foods by trial and error, however, he eventually developed a feeding program that enabled his herd to prosper.

Some herd owners continue to experiment with chin diets today, too, adding their own "secret" ingredients to custom-made pellets. While there may be some differences in the actual feed, there are two practices all successful chinchilla owners follow: (1) they provide a basic diet of prepared pellets, hay, and water; (2) they make dietary changes—if any—slowly.

CHINCHILLA PELLETS

Purchasing good pellets is easy, since there are several types suitable for chinchillas. Commercial chin pellets vary a little in make-up depending upon the brand, but most are basically made from wheat germ, alfalfa meal, oats, molasses, soybean oil meal, corn, vitamins, and minerals. Since the pellets are packaged in 50-pound bags and lose much of their nutritional value within 60 days after being opened, they are not a practical choice for most pet owners. Instead, pet chinchillas are fed rabbit or guinea pig pellets that contain similar ingredients. Guinea pig feed is the recommended choice because of its higher nutritional value and lower fat content, but rabbit pellets are acceptable. An adult is given one to two heaping tablespoons of pellets per day.

If your pet is bright-eyed and active, you'll probably want to continue using whatever pellets it's currently being fed. But if a change is necessary—a brand is no longer available, for instance—mix old and new pellets together for a week or two, gradually increasing the new until the old is completely gone. This gives the animal's digestive tract a chance to adjust to new feed slowly, which is very important to the animal's well-being. Chins are real creatures of habit and will occasionally pick out and eat only the old feed, ignoring the new. However, after it is accustomed to seeing new pellets in the feed dish, the animal will eat them.

Some owners advocate grinding up pellets before giving them to their animals, especially to young stock. Such a practice is not recommended, even for young kits, since chins keep their teeth in shape by chewing on hard surfaces. Hard pellets not only provide nutrition but also actually prevent some dental problems.

HAY

Buying pellets is easy, but purchasing good hay can be a little more difficult. Loose hay can almost always be obtained locally. The problem is that just any old hay won't do. Hay for chinchillas must be harvested from fields that have not been sprayed with chemicals. It must also be dried and cured carefully so that mold can't develop inside the bales, because even the smallest amount of mold can cause major problems. Some animals can tolerate moldy hay, but chinchillas aren't among them. Also, chins can't throw up contaminated feed, so contaminated food, once ingested, will pass through the animal's entire digestive system, wreaking havoc with the chin's health.

Dried, pressed hay cubes, sometimes called mini-bales, are an alternative to loose hay. The cubes, one to two inches long and an inch wide, are made from alfalfa grown in areas with low humidity; they are guaranteed chemical-free and are carefully dried and cured. The hay is pressed into hard blocks, giving the animal another hard surface to shape its teeth on. Like pellets, cubes also are available in 50-pound bags, but the hay cubes will hold their nutritional value a long time if stored in a dry place where mold can't develop. (If stored in a basement or garage, bags of hay should not be placed directly on a concrete floor, where dampness can encourage mold.) Small bags of hay cubes are available through pet stores, and although they may cost more than buying in bulk, they are more practical for a pet owner to use.

An adult chin needs a handful of loose hay or one small mini-bale each day. If the bale is over two inches long, break it into several parts and feed one part each day. A chin can eat only so much hay in a day and will play with the rest, rolling the mini-bale around the cage until there's nothing left. Switching from loose hay to cubes, or vice versa, is not difficult. Chins relish good hay and will gladly eat either form.

A substitute for pet owners allergic to hay may be available from some pet shops. Known simply as hay replacer, it contains both the protein and roughage good hay would provide plus additional vitamins and minerals. Available in 35-pound bags, it, like cubes, will keep for quite a while.

An adult chin needs a tablespoon of replacer per day. It should be placed in its own cup or dish and not mixed in with the pellets. If replacer and pellets are fed together, chins will pick out one to eat and one to throw out, depending upon what their taste buds crave at the moment. Because chins seldom eat anything they've thrown on the floor, a lot of waste can be avoided by using two separate feeding cups.

Add fresh drinking water—an adult needs about a tablespoon a day—and the basic diet is complete.

Besides maintaining a regular diet, owners should also adhere to a regular feeding schedule as much as possible. Usually pellets and hay are given early in the evening when the animal becomes the most active. Water should be available all of the time.

If the chin is going to be left alone for several days, load the feed dish and give hay above and beyond what you would expect the animal to eat during that period of time. The feed will not spoil. This shouldn't become a regular practice, though, since a change in an animal's eating habits is often the first warning sign of illness; when the feed cups are loaded all of the time, it's hard to gauge what an animal is actually eating daily.

FEEDING SUPPLEMENTS

If good pellets and hay are fed, a supplement is not necessary. Sometimes, however, chins need extra nutrition—such as when they are growing rapidly, pregnant or nursing, or recovering from an illness. Besides, part of the fun of owning a pet is giving it extra special care. Supplements are extra and special.

Several supplements, or treats, are available commercially. Gerbil treat would be one example. As long as the treat contains only seeds or pellets for vegetarians, there should be no problem in feeding it.

Supplements can also be homemade. Mix equal parts of wheat germ, powdered milk, rolled oats (either instant or old-fashioned will do), and a baby cereal, or mix equal parts of rolled oats and powdered milk. Both mixes are especially good for babies whose mothers can't provide enough milk for them and for young, rapidly growing animals.

No matter what supplement is chosen, limit a serving to one teaspoonful per day per adult, since too rich a diet results in a fat animal with a short lifespan. Too many helpings of treat will also result in having less hay and pellets eaten; that's a bad development, because both are necessary to the animal's well-being.

Put the supplement in a separate cup or dish if possible when feeding it, or feed pellets and treat about 12 hours apart to avoid mixing. As with hay replacer, if both regular food and treat are fed together, a chin will eat one (the treat in this case) and throw out the others.

Quite a variety of other treats can be given, but one must remember to limit them. It should be an either-or situation, not a little-of-everything smorgasbord. If a chinchilla is given a supplement, other treats are out for the day.

If only one treat is going to be given, make it raisins. Chins simply love them. Feeding one or two several times a week helps prevent constipation, and an "addiction" to them is useful if it ever becomes necessary to administer medication. A drop of an antibiotic on a raisin or a pill hidden inside one is often gobbled down without as much as a sniff at the strange addition.

Chins are also fond of the bark of apple trees, and a few small branches, spray-free, can be given occasionally. Large branches should be cut into chunks. After the animal has stripped the bark, it will gnaw on the wood to trim its teeth. Keep in mind that not every tree bark is harmless; some are poisonous to chins. Use twigs or branches only from fruit trees and then only from those that have seeds, not stones, in the fruit. For example, use pear or mulberry bark, not cherry or plum bark. If you have a mulberry tree, leave some greenery on the twigs and branches. Chins really enjoy mulberry leaves.

Sunflower seeds are not only a treat, they are a beauty treatment as well. Eating a few adds sheen to the animal's fur.

Small pieces of apple (about an eighth of a medium fruit), carrots, or celery can also be given as treats—but not on a daily basis. A chin will gnaw away on such treats slowly. If the animal hasn't finished its fruit or vegetable wedge within a day, be sure to remove it from the cage before mold develops.

Treats should be limited, and there are some items that should be left out of the animal's diet altogether. Extra salt and vitamins are examples.

It used to be a common practice to provide a chin with a salt spool. But unless your pet has a health problem that requires large amounts of salt, there's no need to put one in the cage. Good pellets will provide enough sodium. In addition to being unnecessary, salt spools take on moisture, staining the animal's fur when the pet comes into contact with the spool and its usually rusty holder.

Additional vitamins are another temptation, and water-soluble vitamins are easily added to the animal's drinking water. But here again, unless the pet needs extra vitamins, the practice of doctoring the drinking water isn't recommended. The animal may refuse to drink the strange liquid or drink less than it should. Water containing vitamins can become contaminated more easily than plain water, and a constant watch is needed to avoid bacterial growth. The water also has to be changed often if the vitamins are to maintain their potency.

DIETARY CHANGES

Once in awhile, alterations have to be made in an animal's diet no matter how good the feed is. The easiest way to determine whether change is necessary is to study a chin's droppings. When all is well, the droppings are elongated, firm, and just barely moist. If they are mushy, a dietary change is necessary. Stop all treats and supplements, increase hay, and give the animal a few Wheat Chex or Shredded Wheat biscuits (breakfast cereals). Continue this treatment until the droppings return to normal, usually in two or three days. Should the condition continue or get worse, take away pellets, feed only hay, and check the chapter on disease.

If droppings are limited, hard, dry, and small—the opposite of those described above—check the water supply. Is the animal getting an adequate amount of drinking water? Add several apple, carrot, or celery pieces or a few raisins to the daily diet until normal droppings appear. Take the animal out of the cage for exercise and

The nose of this chinchilla is clean and dry—definitely a good sign.
Photo by Michael Gilroy.

make sure that it moves around. If constipation continues, check the disease chapter.

It's very important not to over-react to temporary diarrhea or constipation. Like ours, a chin's appetite and physical condition can vary from time to time. If the animal's diet was changed too suddenly, if the chin is over-eating (especially common in just-weaned animals), or if the animal is under stress (adjusting to a new home for example), minor health problems can be the result. As long as the animal is active and alert, the situation is not serious; temporary diet modification is often all that is needed to solve the problem.

A final word about droppings: it is not unusual for a healthy animal to eat a few of its own droppings once in a while. It can be upsetting to the owner unless it is understood that such a practice causes no harm. Eating its own droppings helps the chin keep a proper level of "good" bacteria in its digestive system. In fact, a chinchilla recovering from a serious illness during which lots of antibiotics were used may be fed a few ground-up droppings from healthy chins to restore the proper bacterial balance.

Another condition that requires a temporary dietary change is signaled by what is known as "calcium fits." Such seizures almost always occur in young, rapidly growing animals or in pregnant females. True calcium fits are easy to spot. Occurring just before or as soon as the animal starts to eat, the seizures cause the chin to lose its balance and become spastic for several minutes. Although such seizures seldom last more than a few minutes, they can be very frightening. Take the animal from its cage and try to keep it as calm as possible. Don't try to restrain or stop the spastic movements. Simply pet the animal and speak to it calmly. It will be weak for a few minutes after the seizure and then return to its normal antics.

A second kind of fit involves on-going tremors or shaking. It can also be caused by a calcium deficiency, but it may also be a thiamine fit, a nervous disorder, or, in the case of a pregnant female, toxemia. Take the animal to a veterinarian before modifying the diet to make sure the animal is really suffering from a calcium deficiency. It is strongly recommended that you check the veterinarians in your area to locate one experienced in the treatment of chinchillas.

There are several ways to end calcium fits. Add a supplement of powdered milk and rolled oats (50/50) to the animal's diet or purchase calcium lactate in powdered form from your druggist and either sprinkle a little over the pellets or roll raisins in the powder and feed one or two daily. Administer extra calcium for several weeks. Should the seizures return after you've discontinued the supplement program, the animal has a metabolism imbalance, and additional calcium should be given daily.

In cases of severe calcium shortages, a veterinarian can give the animal calcium shots to eliminate the distress. However, the diet should still be modified for the chin's long-term well-being.

Chins are easy, inexpensive, and even fun to feed. They chomp away with enthusiasm and aren't above begging for treats. As long as the owner remembers that a faulty diet—especially one too rich in tidbits—causes most health problems in chins and acts accordingly, that cute pet will thrive.

Both the beige male shown here and the chinchilla on the facing page have eyes and ears in good condition. Photo by Michael Gilroy.

Housing Chinchillas

When Chapman took his chinchillas to California, he not only tried to duplicate the herd's original diet as closely as possible but also tried to recreate its habitat as well. Since his chins had lived in burrows or crevices between boulders, Chapman tried housing his herd in burrows surrounded by large wire pens. He also constructed small oven-shaped concrete houses that were partially buried in the ground to provide quiet, cool, dark places for the animals to live in. A small opening in the back of each house allowed the animals to enter or exit at will, and a large door in the front of the house gave the owner access to his herd.

But burrows and concrete houses weren't practical, and Chapman finally decided to try housing his herd in wire cages. That experiment was eminently successful; more than 50 years later, pets and breeders alike live in similar enclosures.

Each adult chin needs its own cage. Several adult males or adult females can not be housed together—gentle dispositions quickly give way to some nasty displays of temper—and a male and female can not be put in the same cage without a getting-acquainted period. A cage for a single adult should measure at least 16″ wide, 18″ deep, and 12″ high and be made from materials that are rustproof and easy to clean. (Note: *don't* buy a cage with plastic-coated wire. It may be easy to clean, but a chin will chew the plastic off, making a real mess of the cage in the process.)

Unless your plans include breeding chinchillas, the size of the wire mesh (the spacing between the strands of wire) isn't important as long as it's small enough to contain the animal. However, if raising kits is in your plans, the mother's cage must not have openings one inch square or larger or the babies will be able to escape.

Although there are many styles to chose from, the cages themselves fall into only two categories: wire-bottom and solid-bottom. Wire-bottoms allow droppings and loose feed to fall through the openings in the cage floor. Newspapers are placed beneath the cage, usually on a metal sheet (called a drop pan) or piece of plastic, to catch waste. Such cages keep the animal very clean, and because newspapers are used instead of litter as in solid-bottom cages, supplies for wire-bottoms are inexpensive. The papers, however, have to be changed often. A major disadvantage of using a wire-bottom cage is that it can be uncomfortably cool for chins if placed in a drafty location.

Solid-bottom cages are popular with pet owners because they require less work and are more comfortable for the animal. The cage bottom, often a pan that can be pulled out like a drawer for cleaning and filling, is covered with two or three inches of litter such as wood shavings or a moisture-absorbing product like fuller's earth.

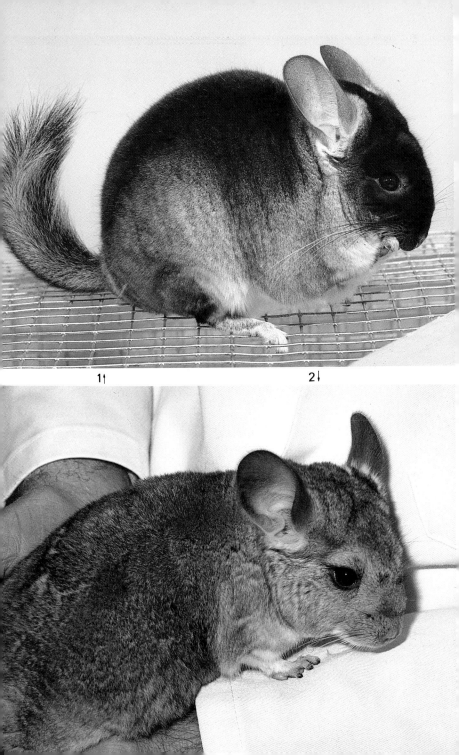

1↑   2↓

1. Black velvet female. 2. Standard gray with coat of poor quality.
3. Pink-white female, spotted with beige. 4. Young charcoal gray male.
Photo #'s 1, 2, 3 by Michael Gilroy. Photo #4 by Vincent Serbin.

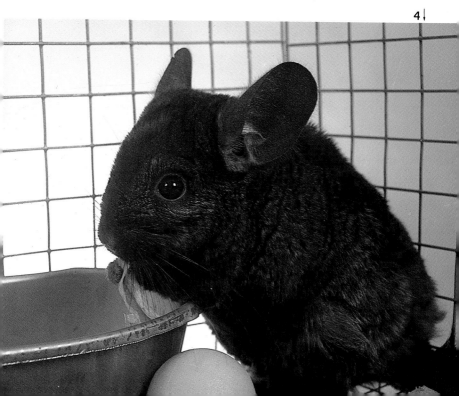

LITTER

Wood shavings are fragrant, inexpensive, easy to obtain—most pet stores carry them—and make a soft bed for the animal. Always keep in mind that your chin might nibble on the litter to see what it tastes like, so don't use shavings that have been treated with chemicals. Some chinchilla breeders use only softwood shavings like pine and caution against using a cedar product if your animal insists on chewing on the litter. Some believe that the resin in cedar shavings may be harmful to chinchillas and urge caution in using them.

Fuller's earth, although not as common, is also used as a litter. It is a white, inert, pebble-like material. After mining, it is dried, crushed, and screened for size before packaging. The most finely ground fuller's earth (60/90 weight) is not suitable for filling cage bottoms since it takes on moisture and is so fine it gets caked in the animal's fur. The coarse mix (8/16 weight) is satisfactory for use as a litter.

One of the major advantages in using fuller's earth is that it can remain in the cage for 30 days before it needs changing, especially if the litter is mixed around often while in the cage.

Fuller's earth is not as readily available as shavings and will probably have to be specially ordered. Because it is so absorbent, it may cause dry skin in some animals. If you use it, watch the animal for excessive scratching and switch to shavings if dry skin appears.

Some cat litters made from ground clay are similar to fuller's earth and could be substituted as long as they haven't been treated with chemicals (including odor neutralizers).

Quite a variety of products have been tested in cage bottoms, but few have proved to be as satisfactory or as safe as shavings. For example, sawdust has been substituted for wood shavings, but it is easily thrown out of the cage when the animal is running around its house, resulting in an empty pan and a mess outside the cage. Ground corn cobs are inexpensive and very absorbent, but the ground cobs can be thrown out of the cage as easily as sawdust and often carry a tiny mite that is not welcome in any household. Sand absorbs moisture from the air while the chin's fur absorbs moisture from the sand, making the animal look messy and feel uncomfortable. Organic products like hay or straw become moldy if left in the cage too long, and when wet they can stain the fur. In short, it can be risky to experiment. Stay with shavings or fuller's earth.

MISCELLANEOUS EQUIPMENT

Besides the cage, your pet needs some basic feeding equipment. A small pellet container is needed, preferably one that hangs on or is fastened to the side of the cage. A glass coaster or heavy dish that won't tip can be used, but as it prances around the cage the animal often scatters the pellets or kicks litter into the dish. If you plan to feed a supplement or hay replacer, more containers are necessary. A coaster can be used for supplement though, as the animal will almost always eat its treat in one sitting.

Holders are available for both loose hay and cubes, but both can be placed directly on the floor of the cage as well. If hay holders are purchased, make sure the animal can get at the hay easily. Some cube holders don't pin the block securely enough, allowing the hay to slide up and away from the animal as it tries to eat.

Chinchillas can drink from coasters, but they often pollute their water with litter and feed. A closed water system is better, and a small bottle with a glass or metal

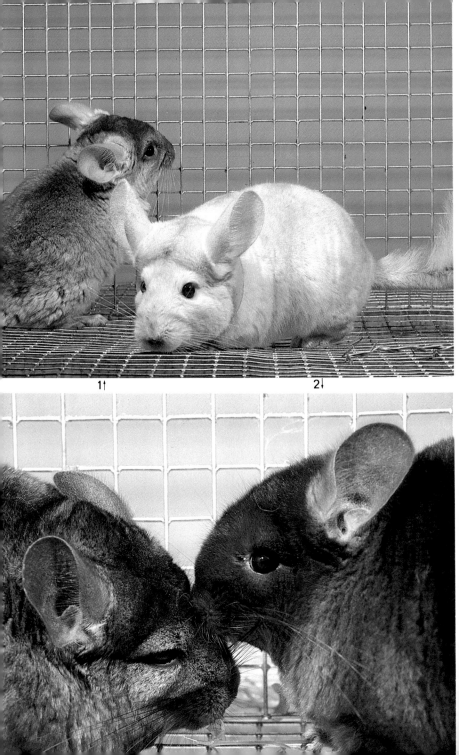

1. Homozygous beige female and brown velvet male. **2.** Charcoal father and his charcoal black son. **3.** Mosaic female. **4.** Closeup of a chinchilla's paws. Photos by Michael Gilroy.

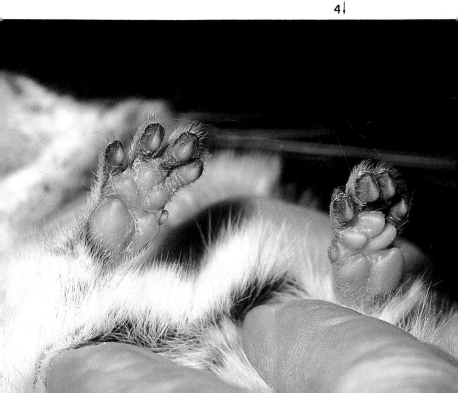

tube—never plastic (the animal will chew it up)—is a good choice. Water bottles and holders are quite varied, and almost any style will work. But if you select a plastic bottle, make sure the holder keeps it in such a position that the animal can't chew a hole in it.

By now it should be obvious that the animal is full of motion and curiosity and that it needs something to do while in the cage. Always provide your pet—no matter what age—with something to chew on, like a piece of wood. A wood block not only helps the animal keep its teeth in shape, it also becomes a useful piece of chin furniture. The animal will sit on the block, sleep on it, or even use it for a pillow. Some make toys out of their blocks, standing them up and running around them, rolling and grinding them into unique shapes, or even picking them up and then dropping them in their feeders over and over again.

Another popular chewing surface is pumice. It can be purchased in big pieces and then sawed into smaller shapes (a four-inch-square piece will last a long time) or purchased in ready-to-use squares known as chew blocks.

There are a number of other items that can be added to your pet's cage.

A large juice can, minus both ends and slightly flattened so it can't roll around easily, makes an ideal place for a small chin to hide or sleep in.

Exercise wheels provide an outlet for the animal's excessive energy.

Heating pads provide luxury. A hard, flat, low-wattage pad made especially for chins can be placed directly *under* one corner of the pan in a solid-bottom cage or held in place with springs *under* a wire-bottom cage. In either type of cage, the pad must be placed and plugged in in such a way that the animal cannot touch any part of it or the cord. A heating pad does not have to be plugged in around the clock. Use it when the animal is ill, the room is drafty or cold, or the animal is sleeping.

A heat lamp placed over one corner of the cage can be substituted for a heating pad. The chin always heads to the warm corner when it's sleeping time.

A thick piece of carpeting can be used to give the animal a soft spot to sleep on and is an especially nice addition if the animal is housed in a wire-bottom cage. Although some of the animals seem to delight in sleeping on the rough backing, most will make good use of the soft pile. A carpet square also gives the animal something more to chew on—most work on the fabric until only shreds are left—and something to play with. They like to move the piece around the cage, flipping and turning it over often. Carpet squares or samples are available at most carpet and flooring outlets and are available at very reasonable prices. One sample cut into 12″ x 12″ pieces will last a chin a year or more.

CAGE LOCATION

The location of the animal's cage is important. Chinchillas thrive in moderate temperatures. Temperatures above 80°F are uncomfortable for them and those above 90°F are dangerous. When selecting a place for the cage, pick an area where it will be cool or where air can be kept on the move if high temperatures occur. Don't place the cage in a position where it will receive lots of sun all day long, and don't put your pet outside in its cage or in an uninsulated garage or attic where temperatures can soar.

Besides the possibility of suffering in high temperatures outdoors, there's another very good reason for not housing your pet outside: its ability to get out of the cage. If it manages to escape in the house, you have

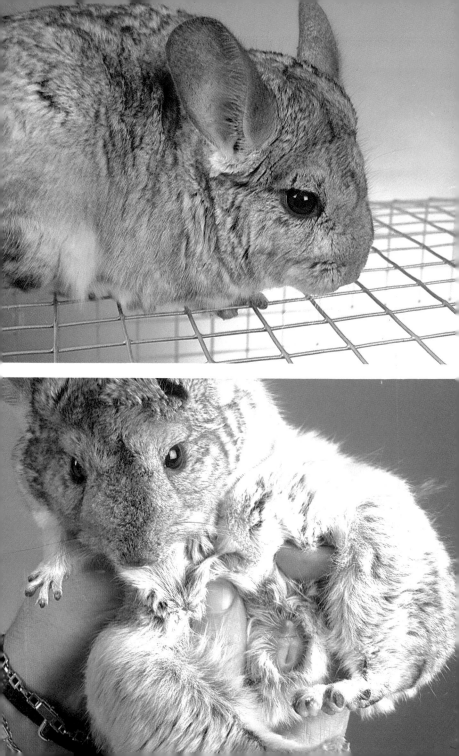

Closeup of genital area of male chinchilla. Photo by Vincent Serbin.

Facing page:
Upper photo: chinchillas are agile and have no difficulty maintaining their balance atop an open wire cage if the grid size of the wires is not too large. *Lower photo:* closeup of the genitalia of a female chinchilla. Photo by Vincent Serbin.

many chances to catch the animal. Outdoors, it will just wander away.

Sometimes even cages and buildings combined aren't enough to keep the pet restrained. One great escape, and now a chinchilla legend, was pulled off by Chapman's herd. Somehow, some of his animals managed to get out of the building where they were being housed. Shortly after discovering the escape, Chapman spotted his chins in a group by some trees, heading back toward a small opening in the building. While that breakout had a happy ending, others haven't. Cats and dogs are well-known for their ability to find their way back home; chins don't have the same reputation. For safety's sake, keep the animal indoors in a cage with a secure closing.

If the room you select for your pet is in use during the day, a cover thrown over the cage will provide the darkness and isolation the chin needs while resting. It can adjust to a number of disturbances quite well. In fact, chinchillas have gone to school to serve as classroom pets and have managed to rest during part of the day even with 30 or more children watching them.

CAGE SANITATION

Keeping the animal's cage clean is easy. The pan or drop pan beneath a wire-bottom cage should be washed when changing litter or newspapers. Soap and water work well, and special cleaners are not necessary unless the animal is sick. During illness, add a little chlorine bleach to the rinse water when cleaning or spray the pan and cage with a disinfectant (follow manufacturer's directions).

Unless the pan or drop pan is made from stainless steel, it will eventually become rusty. To make cleaning easier when that happens, give the pan a coat or two of a rust-proofing paint.

The water bottle should be washed in soap and water once a week. If the animal has been ill, use a *little* chlorine bleach in the rinse water. It is not necessary to add chlorine bleach to the drinking water if the bottle is cleaned often. Chlorine, above and beyond what may be in the drinking water, is sometimes added on large ranches to prevent contamination where watering devices aren't cleaned every week. It is a highly controversial practice since too much chlorine is harmful to a chin. It's much safer to scrub the bottle often and keep it filled with fresh water.

Clean the sides and top of the cage once in a while with a damp rag and use an old bottle brush to pick up any loose hair that gets caught on the wire.

One final tip: wood shavings from the animal's cage make good additions to a gardener's compost pile, and fuller's earth or cat litter helps retain water when small amounts are added to potting soil. Having a chin is not only fun, it could make you a better gardener as well.

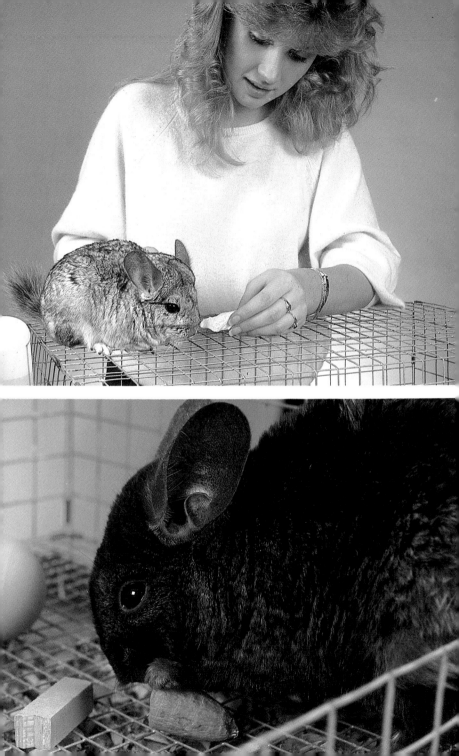

The young lady is properly cradling the body of the chinchilla to give it support. Photo by Vincent Serbin.

Facing page:
Lettuce and carrots can be offered to pet chinchillas on an occasional basis and will usually be accepted, but too much "green" food will be bad. Photos by Vincent Serbin.

Grooming Chinchillas

Chins are almost as easy to keep clean as are their cages. Since they have no noticeable odor and their fur is much too thick—up to 80 hairs per follicle—for insects or parasites to inhabit, chins are not demanding animals to groom. They do, however, need regular baths to get rid of excess moisture and oil in their fur and occasional combings to get rid of loose hair.

Chins bathe not in water but in a finely ground powder, a dust similar to the volcanic ash their ancestors favored in the Andes. Chinchilla bath is available locally but can sometimes be obtained only in bulk. Because it is inexpensive and lasts indefinitely, buying it in large quantities is not a problem.

Put at least two inches of the powder in a container large enough for the animal to roll and flip around in, but small enough to go through the cage door and deep enough to keep the dust in. If too shallow a container is used, the animal will throw the dust out while it cavorts in the bath. Rectangular pans similar to large bread pans or turpentine cans with one broad side cut out and rough edges bent down and under are good choices. A large glass jar placed on its side makes a practical bath because it keeps the dust confined to one area.

When bathing the animal, put the bath in the cage for a limited period of time; five minutes should be adequate. If left in longer, the animal will dig and throw the powder out when it's done bathing no matter how deep or confining is the container. If left in indefinitely, the animal will practically live in the bath, soiling the remaining dust in the process. Besides, it's a rare chin that won't be in the bath before the cage door is closed, and only a few flips and rolls are needed to fluff and clean the fur.

Generally, dusting twice a week is adequate, but if the chin's fur lies down, separates easily as the animal moves, or feels damp to the touch, the animal needs to be bathed more often. During especially humid weather the pet may need a daily bath.

Actually, because chins love to dust, giving a daily bath all year long is tempting and usually not harmful. However, if the animal starts to scratch a lot, too many baths may have resulted in dry skin. Cut back on dusting, and the dry skin condition will improve. If you use fuller's earth for litter in the animal's cage, give fewer baths. The litter and daily baths will almost always lead to a dry skin condition.

The same dust can be reused many times before it needs to be replaced, but do add new dust regularly, keeping several inches of powder in the bath at all times.

Do not substitute other fine powders for chinchilla dust even if they look and feel identical. Such action can cause serious problems. Substituting lime, for instance, can cause death when chins inhale it.

This charcoal male is carefully inspecting fresh greenery before attempting to eat it; chinchillas normally will sniff at and explore all strange foods. Photo by Michael Gilroy.

Facing page:
Upper photo: a chinchilla being offered chinchillas' all-time favorite treat: a raisin. *Lower photo:* like most other rodents, chinchillas like to gnaw, and this chinchilla is being tempted with one of the specially scent-enhanced wooden sticks available at pet shops. Photos by Vincent Serbin.

If fragrance is desired, sprinkle a little talc on the animal outside of the bath and brush it into its fur with your hand. That way it's not breathing in powder that could be harmful to its lungs.

Chinchillas have been shampooed by some owners, but it's a rather tricky and somewhat risky task. For one thing, most chinchillas dislike getting wet and the owner will have a real challenge in getting the animal into a water bath. If you've ever dropped a little water on the animal, you know its instant reaction is to try to get rid of the moisture by wiping it off with a paw or rolling in the cage while scolding in the process. Besides disliking being wet, such a heavily furred animal takes a long time to dry off and risks chilling in the process. Should shampooing be absolutely necessary, use a mild pet soap, tepid water, and lots of towels. Blot the wet fur as thoroughly as possible and finish the drying process with a hair dryer or blower or place the animal over a heating pad or under a heat lamp (making sure the temperature doesn't get too high).

SHEDDING

Don't be alarmed if you suddenly find fluffy balls of loose hair in your pet's cage or uneven fur growth on its back. Chinchillas gradually shed their fur every three months. New fur growth usually starts at the neck and moves slowly like a wave, down the back of the animal and over the sides. Where new hair is pushing up through the old, a distinct line, known as a priming line, can be seen across the animal's back. Shedding occurs just ahead of the slowly moving mark. When new fur growth reaches the tail, the animal is said to be in prime, and its fur is in the best possible condition. A chin will remain like that for several weeks and then begin to grow a new coat all over again.

Not all animals prime the same way. Some seem to grow fur all over all at once, and loose hair is visible everywhere. Others never seem to have priming marks on them, shed very little, and look good all of the time. Still others begin to grow a new coat before the first priming mark reaches the tail.

How an animal primes is thought to be mostly genetic, although weather conditions can influence a priming cycle. Fur ranchers consider the animal's ability to prime properly when selecting breeding stock.

Even without priming lines, it's easy to spot new hair growth: simply blow into the fur. The horizontal white stripe on each new hair just below the gray or black tip, called the "bar," is obvious when it's not even with the old bars and contrasts sharply with the fur closest to the skin, the dark underfur.

COMBING

Regardless of how it primes, a chin needs combing to remove the old fur as it is being shed. This is done not so much for the animal's sake—it will lose the fur whether it is combed out or not—but for the owner's sake. By combing, one can get rid of a lot of loose hair at once and not have it floating around. It also greatly improves the animal's appearance.

Combing requires special tools. Chinchilla combs come in sets of three: a straight-across comb meant for pelts only (unfortunately of no use to a pet owner) and two rounded-edge combs, wide- and fine-toothed.

Cover your lap with an old towel to catch loose hair and protect clothing. On your lap hold the animal by the tail and begin to comb at the tail with the wide-toothed comb, working toward the neck. Use the comb to lift and separate a small section at a time. Continue until all of the back and both sides are combed. It's not

The basic equipmet for a chinchilla cage includes water bottles and holders, feeding dish, a receptacle for holding food supplements, and large and small brushes for cleaning bottles and tubes. Many different varieties of the items shown are available at pet shops. Photo by John A. Zeinert.

Droppings from healthy chinchillas should be firm, elongated, and medium to dark brown in color. There is a noticeable difference in size between the two groups of droppings shown, even though both are from adult animals. Photo by John A. Zeinert.

A chinchilla's basic diet is simple: pellets, hay (either loose or cubed), and water. Photo by John A. Zeinert.

necessary to groom the tummy fur, and don't worry about combing marks. Once the animal shakes itself, they disappear.

When finished, re-groom with the fine-toothed comb to separate the hairs even more and pick up any remaining loose fur.

Combing can be a little difficult at first, especially if the animal is shedding heavily, but it is worth the effort to learn how to do it. Although most animals will struggle when being combed on the back, they do like it around the neck and ears. Sometimes a little combing on the back followed by a few strokes near the neck and then returning to the back again pacifies them.

Don't groom an animal right after dusting. It's actually best to wait a day or two until the dust works its way out of the fur. Excess dusting powder causes the comb to drag on the fur, pulling out hair that isn't loose or dead. It is helpful to comb just before dusting. It helps the powder to penetrate more deeply into the fur to do a thorough job.

If the hair on the tail is too bushy or stained, trim it to your liking with sharp scissors. Simply hold your fingers straight out over the hair, palm facing the tail, and use the outside edges of your fingers as a cutting guide. By placing your fingers between the edge to be cut and the tail, you eliminate any danger of cutting into the tail itself.

That's it. If a chin owner provides a dust bath and gives an occasional combing, the animal will take care of the rest. Chins are tidy creatures by instinct, and even little kits can be seen clipping their nails and licking their paws to wash behind their ears or clean their whiskers. A chin is simply a neat pet and easy to keep that way.

Common Health Problems

Chinchillas are usually healty, robust animals, and if fed properly and housed in a clean environment they should remain that way. However, because chins, like any animal, are exposed to ever-present bacteria and fungi, they can become ill. This chapter has two purposes: to identify the most common health problems and to recommend treatment should any occur.

The earlier an ailment is identified, the easier it is to treat. Make a practice of really looking at your pet every day. Does the animal have bright, shiny eyes? Is it eating well? Is it active and alert? If the answers to those questions are "yes," all is well. But if the answer to even one of those questions is "no," the animal should be examined carefully. It may be sick.

Dull, watery eyes are a warning sign that all is not well. If the "weeping" is accompanied by red and swollen lids or white matter surrounding the eye, the animal's eye is infected. The infection may be a simple one resulting from dust or small pieces of litter in the eye, or it might be the result of lowered resistance due

This cage has alternative cage gates, allowing its use in a polygamous breeding program; here the cage gate is being inserted into the male's run. Photo by Michael Gilroy.

Chinchillas enjoying their dust bath in a cat litter pan. Photos by Vincent Serbin.

to stress or improper diet allowing infectious bacteria to get the upper hand. In either case, it's off to the veterinarian for you and your chin.

Take a small bath towel along to the doctor's to restrain the animal during its examination. Wrapping the chin in the towel so only the pet's head shows calms the animal and keeps those little paws out of the way.

The doctor will probably prescribe an ophthalmic medication, usually a petroleum-jelly-like ointment, and show you how to clean and medicate the eye. In advanced cases, the doctor may also recommend administering a broad-spectrum antibiotic.

Clean and disinfect the animal's cage with chlorine bleach and, if using a solid-bottom cage, cover the bottom with an old, clean towel rather than litter. Otherwise, once treated the animal will try to get rid of the eye ointment by rolling around in the cage, picking up pieces of litter around and even in the eye in the process.

Clean and disinfect the dust bath container, too, and fill it with fresh powder, but don't dust the animal until the infection is gone and you've stopped medicating the eye.

Eye infections may seem hopelessly advanced when discovered yet respond very well to modern medications. It will take several days of cleaning and medicating, but significant progress should be noted in three to four days.

Watery eyes without infection may indicate a cold or the onset of pneumonia. Check the animal to see if it's running a temperature. The surest way to determine temperature is to use a special thermometer made for small pets. A chin's normal temperature is the same as a human's, 98.6°F. The easiest way to determine elevated temperature is to examine the animal's ears. If warm to the touch and bright pink or even red, the animal is probably running a temperature. However, sometimes an animal sleeps on its side in such a way that an ear is snuggled down in the litter and becomes flushed from the extra warmth. If the animal becomes active after waking up and the bright color disappears, its temperature is normal. But if the high color remains and the animal is listless, listen to its breathing. A stuffy head indicates a cold; wheezing or difficulty in breathing may indicate pneumonia.

To treat a cold, keep the animal warm and make sure it has lots of water to drink. Don't dust it until the condition clears up. Watch the pet closely for complications that may indicate the onset of pneumonia.

To treat pneumonia you will need a vet's assistance and antibiotics. Given a choice, ask for a sweetened (preferably cherry-flavored) medication. It will be much easier to administer than anything with a bitter or sour taste.

MEDICATIONS

Liquid medications are given to the animal by a dropper. Start by putting a few drops on the animal's lower lip. Usually it will lick the drops off its mouth and, if it likes the taste, will take the rest from the dropper without too much of a struggle. *Never* force the liquid into the animal's mouth. It may go into the lungs, compounding the problem.

Should the animal resist, continue to put the dropper to its mouth until the pet understands that you won't give up until the medicine is gone.

When a pill is prescribed, hide it in a raisin or crush the tablet and roll the raisin in the powder, feeding it as a "treat."

This commercially available standard wire chinchilla cage is roomy and offers good protection to the chinchilla; the bottom tray is removable for ease in changing the litter. Photo by Vincent Serbin.

Facing page:
Upper photo: Almost any deep container big enough to hold a chinchilla and several inches of dust will be adequate for a chinchilla bath. *Lower photo:* A wire-bottom cage like the one shown is easy to clean. Photo by John A. Zeinert.

Don't accept or rely on any medication that is added to the animal's drinking water or sprinkled over its feed. It may be a lot easier to dispense than drops or pills, but it's seldom very effective since sick chins usually stop eating and drink very little. The owner must accept the responsibility for putting the medicine in front of the animal and seeing that it takes it.

Besides giving it medication, keep a pneumonia-stricken chin warm and as quiet as possible. If it's not drinking, try giving it water via the dropper several times a day. Usually progress can be noted in three to four days.

TOOTH CARE

Besides signaling infection or pneumonia, watery eyes could also be a sign of tooth problems. Watch the animal eat. Does it paw at its mouth while chewing or have a wet chin due to drooling? Are the front teeth so long that the animal can't close its mouth properly? Is the animal just "skin and bones"? If the answers are affirmative, the animal has serious dental problems.

Before trying to cure a dental problem, you may want to have your pet's mouth X-rayed by your veterinarian. If front teeth are the only problem, they can be clipped (a very sharp nail clipper will work) into shape and re-clipped when necessary. Far too often, though, the back teeth, which are almost impossible to work on, are irregular in shape as well. Sometimes the back teeth will develop spurs that grow downward into the lower jaw or upward toward the eyes, occasionally entering the eye sockets. There is no permanent cure for dental problems in chins. If the problems are advanced, the animal will not be able to eat properly. Furthermore, it will experience pain from the developing spurs. It is best to put the animal to sleep to avoid unnecessary suffering.

Tooth problems, when they do occur, are often the result of old age or the result of the animal lacking something to chew on. An ounce of prevention in the shape of a wood block or pumice stone can help avoid such problems.

FUNGUS

Another ailment that affects chins and may be accompanied by watery eyes is known simply as fungus. While it appears most often during hot, muggy weather, it can show up anytime.

One form of fungus causes the fur to fall out in patches, exposing irritated skin beneath that is either bright pink or red in color. Usually fur losses occur around areas where moisture is present, such as the eyes and nose, but they can appear anywhere.

The other type of fungus causes fur breakage that results in patches of thin, shaggy hair. Often the animal's whiskers will be split, broken, or bent at the ends. One side may be affected but not the other.

In either case, change the dust in the animal's bath and add a heaping tablespoon of a foot powder for athlete's foot, mixing the powder into the dust. One tablespoon of one of the powders used for fungus control in gardens can be mixed into the dust instead, but since some people are very sensitive to the powder it should be used only for short periods of time.

Purchase a small bottle of Grifulvin® from your druggist. Put a drop or two of the medication on a raisin and give one to your pet in the morning, another in the evening for three or four days. Chins like the sweet taste of Grifulvin® and will gladly take their medicine.

Skin irritation should disappear within a few days. The red or bright pink color should be replaced with

Combing the chinchilla can be pleasurable for both owner and pet. Photo by Vincent Serbin.

Facing page:

Upper photo: The correct color of an adult chinchilla's incisors is as shown here, yellow to yellow-orange. Photo by Michael Gilroy. *Lower photo:* The tail can easily be trimmed and shaped with the aid of a sharp scissors. Photo by John A. Zeinert.

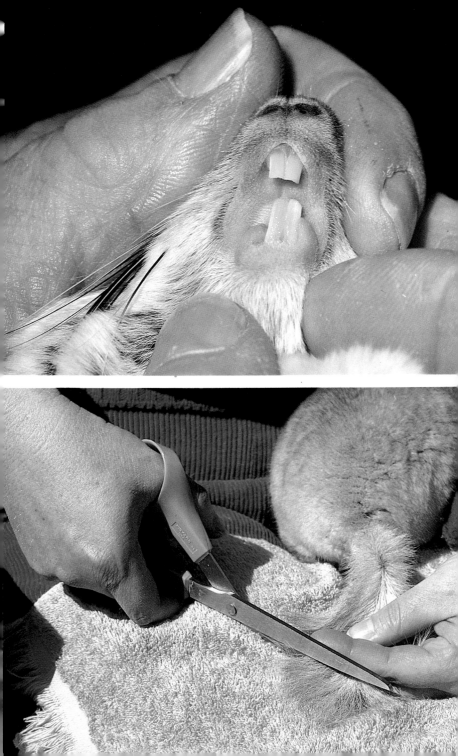

gray or white, and new fur should begin to appear within a week.

In the case of broken fur, it will take longer to notice an improvement since the old broken fur will still complete its growth cycle before being replaced by new hair.

If you live in an area with warm temperatures and high humidity all year long, you may want to add athlete's foot powder—but not garden fungus powder—to the animal's dust bath regularly as a preventive.

Not all fur damage is caused by fungus; some chins nip on their own hides. Examine the fur carefully before assuming the damage is caused by fungus and administering unnecessary medication. If the damaged area has a crew-cut look or is wet or matted, the animal has probably been chewing on it.

FUR CHEWING

Although studies have been conducted for years as to why a few chins chew and many others don't, it's still not clear what causes an animal to eat its own fur. Some chin owners believe there is a genetic factor involved— and there's lots of support for this theory—while others believe the chewing is a result of a protein-poor diet. Some ranchers note that a chin will chew under stress but once the tension-producing event is over—like attending a show or being moved to a new home—the chewing will stop. Although it is not a threat to the animal's health, it certainly doesn't help the animal's appearance, and fur producers are anxious to determine what causes chewing.

EAR AILMENTS

Ear ailments are not as common as watery eyes and are usually the result of another infection or the result of lowered resistance due to a poor diet. If you spot drainage from the animal's ear, see the chin paw at an ear often, tip its head to one side repeatedly, or walk around in circles, take the animal to a veterinarian as soon as possible.

The doctor will clean the ear and administer an antibiotic, usually through drops in the pet's ear. Your vet will also tell you how and for how long to continue medication.

Disinfect the cage. If it has a solid bottom, use a towel rather than litter to cover the floor of the cage. Keep the chin warm and as quiet as possible. Don't dust the animal until it is well and off medication.

BACTERIAL INFECTIONS

Diarrhea or constipation are usually temporary conditions controllable by dietary changes. However, if either condition lasts for more than a few days, worsens, or is accompanied by droppings coated with mucus or stuck together in long strings surrounded by a jelly-like substance with air bubbles, the animal has more than simple diarrhea or constipation. It may, in fact, have enteritis. Watch the animal's activities. If it refuses to eat, shows no interest in treats, sits in a "hunched-up" position, or loses its balance when it tries to walk, it definitely needs medical attention as soon as possible.

Since different bacteria can cause various forms of enteritis, tests may be required to determine which culprit is causing the problem. Take some droppings along to the vet's for possible analysis.

Unless a specific bacterium can be identified, the veterinarian will probably recommend a broad-spectrum antibiotic. Follow the doctor's directions carefully.

Keep the animal warm. While it is recovering, give it water by the dropper to make sure it gets enough liquid and feed it plenty of hay.

If you lift a chinchilla while playing with it, be sure to support it by keeping your hands either around (but not too tight) or under the animal. Photo by John A. Zeinert.

Facing page:

Upper photo: The twins shown here are a handful for their mother, and scrapping is common. The babies have to be removed from the cage periodically to be handfed and to give their mother a rest. Photo by John A. Zeinert. *Lower photo:* If the animal refuses to face you, simply scoop it up from behind with one hand and steady it by grasping the tail with the other. Photo by John A. Zeinert.

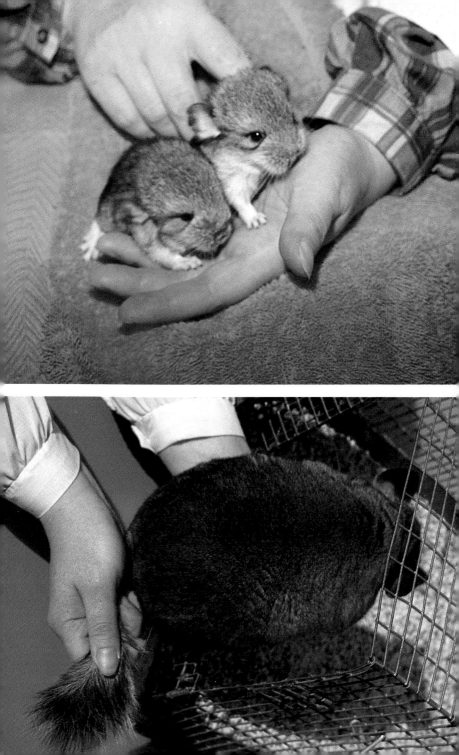

In cases of constipation, try to get the animal to exercise. One technique is to give the chin a dust bath several times a day and let it roll around in the powder as long as it wants. Another technique is to take it from its cage, put it on the floor, and prod it along gently, forcing it to move.

Animals treated for long periods of time with antibiotics—such as pneumonia patients and enteritis victims—often need help to restore helpful bacteria in their digestive tracts once medication has ceased. A product called acidophilus will aid in restoring the proper balance. Mix a little of the liquid (local grocery or health food stores may carry it) with yogurt (rumor has it that blueberry is a favorite with chins) and give it by the dropperful.

Unless the chin's cage is in a poor location, heat prostration should not be a problem. When a heat wave occurs, put the animal somewhere where air is circulating, preferably in the coolest room in the house, and give the pet lots of fresh, cool water to drink. Should the animal be overcome by heat and lying on its side gasping for air or even in a coma, immerse the animal in cool—not cold—water up to its neck to lower its temperature.

Cuts and bruises are seldom problems for pet chins because they live in very protected environments. But when more than one chin shares a cage, some roughhousing or even plain fighting might occur. Minor cuts or scratches simply need cleaning and time to heal. Panalog®, available through your vet, is the most commonly used ointment for treatment of more serious cuts or minor infections.

If your animal experiences "fits" or "seizures" when it begins to eat, its diet needs to be modified. Read the chapter on feeding again.

Proper diet and a clean environment are the key elements needed to keep your chin healthy. Many ranchers would add another factor—absence of stress. Stress caused by extreme temperature changes, rough handling, or rapid changes in diet lowers the chin's resistance to disease and allows harmful bacteria to get the upper hand. In fact, some sources believe that stress is the major cause of chinchilla disease and death.

Be sure to make any changes in the animal's diet gradually and give it plenty of time to adjust to its new home and surroundings before you begin to play with it. By eliminating stressful situations, a chin owner increases tremendously the animal's chances of living a long, healthy life.

VACCINATIONS

A final note regarding illness: chinchillas can be vaccinated by an all-in-one vaccine at any age against the most dangerous diseases they might encounter. The animal initially receives two shots seven days apart, followed by an annual booster (Kline Chinchilla Res. Found.). You'll need a vet's help in obtaining the vaccine and administering the shots. Usually pets aren't vaccinated simply because they're not exposed to as many diseases as are animals raised on large ranches, where animals travel to and from shows often or where new breeding stock is added on a regular basis. However, vaccination is a precaution that greatly cuts the odds on disease in chinchillas and one that pet owners might want to consider. Just as you would discuss your dog's or cat's vaccination program with your vet, the entire problem of vaccinations for chinchillas should be resolved by discussions with your veterinarian.

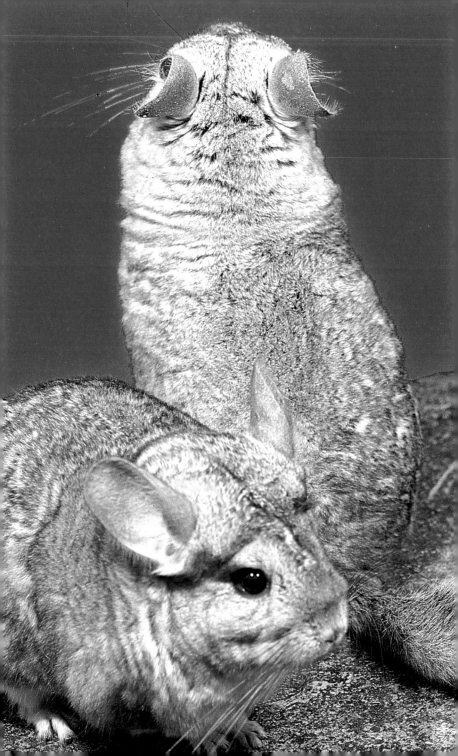

Facing page:
The luxuriant, plush coat of the chinchilla is obvious here. Photo by Michael Gilroy.

Above: These dark beige males are from the same litter and result from the breeding of a standard mother and a beige father. *Below:* Homozygous beige chinchillas like the one shown have light red, almost pink, eyes. Photos by John A. Zeinert.

Playing with Chinchillas

Chinchillas can make interesting playmates, but it's important that a new pet be given some time to get acquainted with both its surroundings and the owner before being handled a lot.

If the new pet shows fear, it's probably best to start the getting-acquainted period by playing with the chin in its cage. Simply put your hands in the cage without trying to catch or handle the animal. The chin's curiosity will overcome its apprehension, and it will approach you to sniff and taste and, eventually, to sit on your hands. After a moment or two it will run to a corner of the cage but will quickly return to recheck its findings.

End the first play periods with a small treat so the animal learns to associate good things with your hands. (Don't start the getting-acquainted periods with a tidbit like raisins or the chin will spend all of its playtime looking for more treats. Also, because your hands will smell like raisins, the chin may bite them.)

Once the animal is willing to sit on your hands, it should be easy to catch it. It may even come out on its own if a pair of hands, palm side up, await it in front of the cage's open door. As the chin becomes more secure, it will turn hand-sitting into arm-crawling, venturing farther and farther outside the cage door. It may be a little ego-deflating to realize that the animal is just as interested in what's outside the cage as he or she is in you, but it is normal for the animal to want to explore its surroundings.

The intelligence level of a chinchilla is said to be comparable to that of a squirrel's, and if you've ever tried to outwit a squirrel at a bird feeeder, you know that intelligence is considerable. Therefore, chins have the ability to be trained to do a variety of things including speaking, begging for treats, and answering to a name.

One way to reinforce the lessons you choose to teach is to reward the animal with a raisin or a sunflower seed. Another reinforcement is to pet and cuddle the animal. Chins like to be scratched behind the ears and under the neck. Some actually get so spoiled that they tip their heads to one side or hang their heads out of the cage as soon as the door is opened, hoping for attention.

How you train and play with your chin will depend in large part upon its personality. Chins may look alike but they don't necessarily act the same. One pet owner, who got started in chinchillas after her teacher bought a small herd for a sixth grade science project, owned several chins at one time and was able to note significant differences in their behavior. One chin liked to play with her owner, pushing fingers away when they were pointed at her and demanding attention. Another was too independent to sit with his owner very long and preferred to explore the house instead. A third came when called and had a favorite perch, the back of the sofa. Although the animals had been treated alike, their actions varied. In short, while an owner is trying to decide what

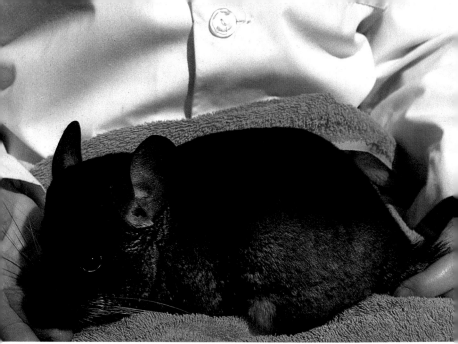

1. It usually takes as long as a year for a black mutation like this one to grow all of its mutant fur. Most blacks appear to fade out shortly after birth, becoming black again when they grow their adult fur. **2.** A young chinchilla like this one needs to be handled especially carefully. Small children should be watched carefully so that they don't squeeze the animal. **3.** Branches, pumice stone, wood blocks—all used by chinchillas to keep their constantly growing teeth in shape. Not all branches are equally safe. **4.** Wrapping the chinchilla in a towel calms the animal and makes it easier for the owner to administer medication. Photos by John A. Zeinert.

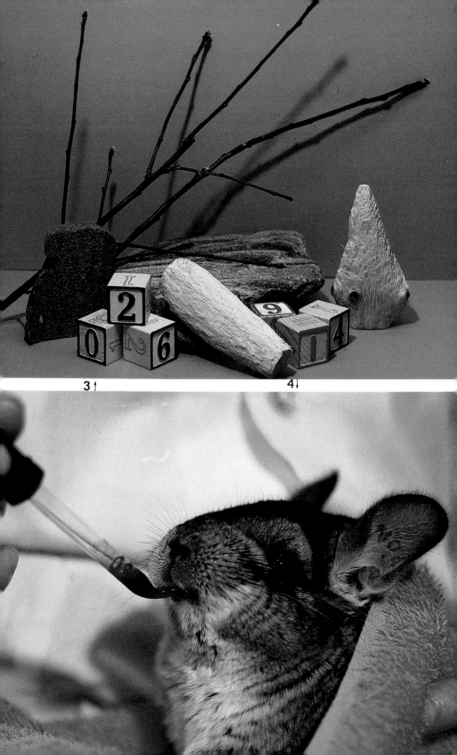

2

3 ↑   4 ↓

the pet should do, he or she must also consider the pet's ability and temperament.

A chin's age should also be taken into consideration when trying to train it or play with it since it goes through some very definite stages as it matures. Very young kits, those less than three weeks old, are quite apprehensive about being caught or held. It's best to work with such an animal in the cage. It will gladly sit on your hand or nibble on your fingers if its mother is close by. It will also follow its mother's example. If she is calm when you touch her, the baby will tend to react the same way.

When a chin is close to weaning, six to eight weeks old, it is very willing to come out of the cage but will almost always struggle to get away. Its attention span is very short, and it just wants to look at and taste everything right away. Even hungry hand-fed kits will run away half way through their feeding if given a chance.

Once weaned, chins seem to settle down a little. They are more confident and are much easier to make into pets than are new kits.

That doesn't mean that very young animals shouldn't be touched. The more familiar an animal is with its owner, the easier it will be to make a playmate out of it. The trick in successfully working with a chin is to respect its various growing stages and not rush the animal. It's a rare two-week-old kit that can be taught to come when called and a rare six-month-old chin that won't do almost anything for a raisin.

It's all right to take your chin outside to play on a cool, sunny day if you take several precautions. First of all, make sure that the chin doesn't get too warm. Move indoors immediately if the animal's ears become flushed or the pet starts to breathe heavily or wants to lie on its side.

This homemade baby creep has two inches of clearance between the top and bottom and an inch and a half of space between the nails. The hinged top allows access to the feed cup inside, making it ideal for feeding supplement to babies. The edges of the creep are protected by metal strips to prevent the chinchillas from making shavings out of them. Photo by John A. Zeinert.

Secondly, select a play area that's fenced in. If suddenly frightened by strange noises, a neighbor's dog, or even shadows, a chin will instinctively run for cover and away from its owner.

Furthermore, be forewarned that the great outdoors isn't the place to try to teach your pet new tricks. The surroundings are new to the animal and would be a distraction. In fact, trying to teach a chin outdoors would just be an exercise in frustration for both of you.

Go outside with the chin when you both want to sit in the sun for awhile and just enjoy a nice day together. It's a pleasant place to play with your chin.

Chinchillas are a lot like people when it comes to taking medications. Sour or bitter-tasting medicines will make them pucker up and turn away, but chins will take medicine from a dropper without too much difficulty if they like the taste. (Cherry and molasses flavors are high on their list of favorites.) Photo by Vincent Serbin.

Above: A family group. *Below:* A standard medium male. Photos by Michael Gilroy.

Breeding Chinchillas

The first chinchilla owners needed offspring to increase their herds. To minimize risk, they tried to maintain mating practices of the wild chinchilla. It was assumed that chins had bonded with one mate in the Andes, so for years pair mating was practiced here. As numbers of progeny were produced, they were paired for selling, which reinforced the practice.

Eventually pair mating was questioned, challenged, and changed just as old dietary and housing practices had been. Ranchers began to experiment with polygamous units, and chins once again proved to be adaptable. The harem system prospered. A polygamous breeding arrangement allowed ranchers to raise more animals at a lower cost since fewer males were required. It also resulted in a trickle of reasonably priced animals—usually surplus males—into the pet market.

Pet owners who choose to breed chinchillas seldom want the number of offspring a polygamous system might produce. Instead, they step back in time to breed chins in pairs as Chapman did.

SEXING CHINCHILLAS

If breeding chins is in your plans, start by double-checking your pet's sex before shopping for your chin's mate. Sometimes it is difficult to classify newborns, and if the former owner recorded the sex at birth without re-checking, it might be incorrectly identified. Even experienced ranchers have been known to make mistakes.

It's easier to sex a chinchilla if you have one of each side by side for comparison, but by examining the pet carefully you should be able to classify it. If the animal is a female, the anus and clitoris will be very close together and a horizontal slit, the vaginal opening, will sometimes be just noticeable in between. If the animal is a male there will be a considerable separation between the anus and penis.

BREEDING FOR COLOR

Besides determining the sex of the prospective mate, the pet owner may have a choice between breeding a standard to another standard or mating a standard to a mutation. Because mutations are not as readily available—fewer are raised and the most unusual colors are very expensive—only the most common (beige, black, and white) will be mentioned here. It's important that the owner understand what the results will be before he or she breeds the animals.

All three are classified as incompletely *dominant mutations*. That is, when bred to standards, half of the offspring should be the same color as the mutant parent—beige, black, or white—and half should be standard. (Some of the white offspring may not be a solid white. The pair may also produce a mosaic or a white with a few to a lot of gray hairs mixed in. When enough gray hairs are present, the animal is known as a silver.) In

A chinchilla in one of its favored poses—nibbling a treat. Photo by Vincent Serbin.

Facing page:
Upper photo: Most chinchilla ranchers have a grading table, show lights, and show cages so that they can evaluate their animals before putting them into breeding runs. The chinchillas shown here have already been evaluated for an upcoming show. The rancher will record their birthdates and ranch numbers on a form so as to have the information available for registration at the show. The chinchillas' ears will be marked with a felt-tipped pen to identify them; the rancher's brand will be put in one ear and the animal's number in the other. Photo by John A. Zeinert.

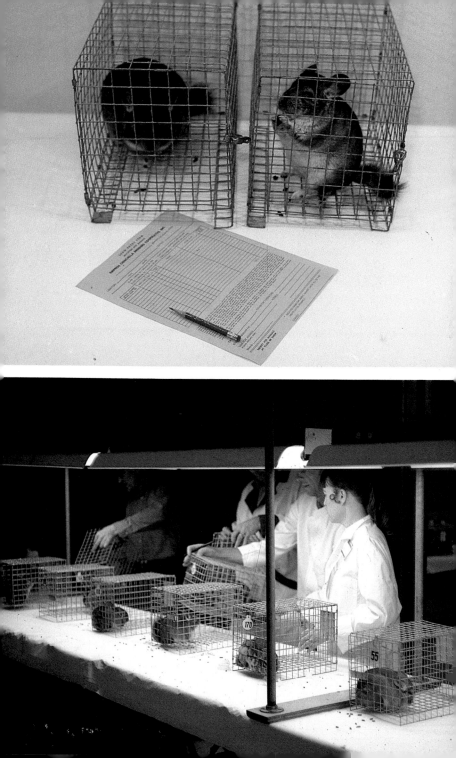

short, dominant does not mean that all of the progeny will carry the mutant coat color. Furthermore, it must be remembered that the percentages are figured on a large number of animals. It's quite possible to have three or four litters consisting of all standard or all mutation offspring. If enough litters are produced, the coat color should average out. There are, to further complicate matters, some animals that seem to produce larger or smaller numbers of mutations than the anticipated average. (We currently have two beige male breeders, a father and his son. One has sired a larger than average number of beige offspring; the other beige male, his son, hasn't fathered a single beige in eight litters.) Don't automatically assume you'll be able to produce mutations because you have a mutant breeder. It may take several litters to get the color you want.

Mutations can be bred to other mutations. If a white and a beige are mated one of three types of offspring could be born: standard (both parents carry standard in their background regardless of their coat color); white (which might be creamy, spotted, or pure white); or beige.

A beige and a black pairing could produce several different colors: black; beige; standard (again, both parents carry standard in their background); or touch-of-velvet beige, a dark beige with a velvety brown head and grotzen.

A black and white combination could produce white (not necessarily solid white); black; or standard kits.

Although beiges are bred to other beiges to produce purebreds for color (homozygous beiges), blacks and whites are not bred to chins with the same coat color. A lethal factor appears to be present, and fewer babies are born to such parents.

Breeding *recessive mutations*, such as charcoals, sapphires, or violets, can be as interesting as working with dominants. One recessive is bred to another of the same coat color to produce the mutant color. Therefore, two charcoals, two sapphires, or two violets will produce offspring identical in coat color to the parents, at least in theory. But, if a recessive is bred to a standard, all of the offspring will appear to be standards. Some of the progeny, though again in theory, should carry the recessive color gene. It is only through breeding such animals and evaluating their offspring that an owner can tell whether or not they are carriers. Two recessive carriers when bred together should/will eventually produce a recessive kit with the desired coat color.

Because pet owners seldom have the necessary number of animals to work with recessive carriers to avoid excessive inbreeding, breeding such animals is probably best left to large ranchers.

Chinchilla genetics is a fascinating topic, and new coat colors appear every once in a while. Often though, the new mutation is a weak animal with poor fur quality, and it takes generations of selective breedings to improve the new mutation's qualities to the point where it is desirable for breeding stock.

INTRODUCING THE PAIR

No matter what color the chins are, a male and female can not be housed together without a getting-acquainted period. The couple-to-be should be put in separate cages side by side so they can communicate with and "sniff at" each other. Even though we can't smell a chinchilla, each has a scent that is identifiable by other chins, and mates need to become familiar with it before being put in the same cage.

Chinchilla shows offer opportunities for recognition and various forms of awards such as these trophies and ribbons. Photo by John A. Zeinert.

Allow at least one week for an introduction period. Then, when putting the male in the female's cage, plan to watch their activities carefully. *FAILURE TO DO SO COULD RESULT IN SERIOUS INJURIES OR EVEN DEATH.*

At first the male will probably be more interested in the cage than in his prospective mate, and it's quite common for him to check out all four corners and even gnaw away on chew blocks before acknowledging her. She, on the other hand, will be very interested in the intruder and will follow him around the cage.

Once he's checked out the cage, a little rough-housing may take place as the two take turns chasing each other around. They may pause from time to time to chew on each other's ears and nibble the fur around their mate's eyes as they try to decide whether the prospective spouse is suitable. The chewing may look rough, but unless it turns to blood-letting biting the animals seem to enjoy it.

If the male or the female becomes overly aggressive and nibbling turns to attacking or "hacking away" at the other chin so that the fur literally flies, separate them immediately.

When the female does the rejecting, she usually doesn't use her teeth, at least not at first. She will instead aim her clitoris and shoot urine at the intruder. (She can do this to humans, too, aiming for the eyes.) As soon as the female puts her back into the corner and rears up on her hind legs to give the male a shower, it's time to separate them.

Another week of being side by side should lessen the fear and hostility expressed by the animals. Chins seldom reject a prospective mate completely, but if it does happen there is no choice but to replace one of them, preferably the more aggressive animal.

Once acceptance has been achieved, there is seldom a serious hassle between the two until the female comes into heat and sometimes not even then.

A female chinchilla is able to breed at approximately seven to eight months of age. She will come into cycle about every 30 to 40 days, but this doesn't mean that she's always willing to breed then. In fact, until chinchillas feel secure in their surroundings, they will not reproduce.

An alert chin owner can tell when the female is approaching her most receptive period. The male will become much more attentive, sniffing, and nuzzling, sometimes wagging his tail, and even vocally communicating his desire to mate. Shortly before the female is ready to breed, a small whitish, waxlike "plug" will be ejected from the vagina. Sometimes the plug is visible in the cage; more often than not, it is mixed in with the litter or eaten by one of the animals.

As her mating time approaches, the male will become more aggressive and some roughness might occur simply because the male is ready long before the female will accept him. While some males are willing to bide their time, others become very aggressive and may have to be removed for a few hours or even a day until the female is more willing.

If a large juice can is used in the cage as a hide-away and a toy, remove it when you see mating attempts or the female may choose to hide inside it until her conception period is over.

When a breeding attempt has taken place, the male will emit a cry best described as a hiccuping sound. He will also emit a wax-like substance during copulation that will harden to temporarily retain the semen in the vagina.

After a breeding attempt has taken place, check the male to make sure he is able to withdraw his penis back into the protective foreskin. Occasionally an inexperienced male develops a "hair ring" around his penis during copulation and is unable to remove the hair himself. Remove the hair manually, using petroleum jelly as a lubricant if necessary. Unless redness and swelling occur (signs of infection and the need for medication), nothing more needs to be done.

The male and female may remain in the same cage until the babies arrive.

POST-BREEDING PREPARATIONS

Count off 111 days on the calendar and circle that date for the litter's arrival. Chins are remarkably predictable for delivery purposes, seldom varying more than a day or two.

Modify the female's diet by increasing pellets and hay as the need arises and provide a commercial supplement or a homemade mix of equal parts of rolled oats, powdered milk, wheat germ, and a baby cereal daily.

About half way through the pregnancy the female may go off her feed for a few days and may even lose weight in the process. This is not a cause for alarm and should not be treated as a health problem unless other warning signs of disease are present.

The temptation to check for weight gain or swelling is great, but don't handle the female while she is carrying. Should damage occur to the fetuses through careless handling by the owner during the first 60 days of pregnancy, the fetuses may die and the female, rather than aborting, will absorb the matter back into her system. Some chin owners believe that a number of babies are lost this way. To be on the safe side, don't take the mother-to-be out of the cage anymore than is absolutely necessary.

Instead, busy yourself with preparations for the coming litter. If you don't have a heating pad for the cage, you might want to buy one now. A pad is invaluable in helping to dry off newborns, who are heavily furred and soaking wet. Expectant mothers appreciate the extra warmth on their tummies and seem more relaxed and comfortable than those without a heating element. Wire-bottom cages require a heating pad or a flat surface like a large piece of carpeting where the wet babies will be protected from drafts beneath the cage since any draft when the kit is wet is magnified, and chilling is a real threat to a kit's well-being.

In addition, the heating pad provides a warm place for the babies to sleep by themselves, giving the mother a chance to get away from the responsibility of keeping them warm. With a heating pad present, a mother is often found taking a break in another corner of the cage while her babies snuggle above their artificial heat source.

It's also practical to prepare a special place for the babies to hide if both parents are to remain in the same cage. Known as a baby creep, such a hideaway might be as simple as a small, slightly flattened—to keep it from rolling—juice can with both ends removed or an elaborate creep complete with a feeding dish. Regardless of the type of creep, it should be so small the parents can't get in, especially if you plan to feed a supplement to the babies and you don't want the mother or father to eat it. The feed cup must be located far enough inside the creep so that even the narrowest head or the longest tongue of an adult chin can't get close enough to the dish to clean it out. Kits love it and use the creep until they are so big they have to squeeze in to enter.

Before the litter arrives, the mother's cage should be checked for any openings where babies might escape even if the mesh is very small. If the feed dish hangs on the side of the cage, check the opening where you feed. *ANY* opening larger than one inch by one inch will provide an exit for an active kit, and a healthy baby *WILL* find it. Baby chinchillas are just as curious as their parents, and once their cage is thoroughly scouted they will try to move on to more exciting vistas. Once out of the cage, they can become chilled and die. Even day-old kits are strong enough to pull the escape routine. Secure that cage!

THE BIRTH PROCESS

A few days before the expected delivery, the mother-to-be will eat less and drink more. Soft droppings are not uncommon and not a cause for concern. The female will stretch often and lie around more than usual.

Shortly before delivery she will stretch a great deal and fluid will be released from the sac surrounding the babies.

As labor progresses, contractions will become very obvious. The babies should appear within two to three hours. Should labor take longer than four hours or if contractions stop altogether before a litter is born, the female needs prompt medical attention. It is not common for a female chin to experience great difficulty during delivery, and the vast majority of kits are born without complications.

An average litter consists of two—the national average is 1.9—but as many as eight have been born in one litter.

The mother will quickly remove each kit's sac and clean and then dry the kits with her fur. When the placenta or afterbirth arrives, she may eat it. Some ranchers believe that allowing the female to eat the afterbirth will increase milk flow; others remove it as soon as it appears in the cage. In short, there's no common practice here.

After all contractions have stopped, check the female to make sure she's delivered all of the babies and all placentas (one for each kit) by gently palpating the abdominal area. An undelivered kit or placenta will feel like a firm mass.

If you suspect that a kit has not been delivered, take the animal to a veterinarian. The vet can verify your findings and give the animal an injection to induce labor if necessary.

It is unusual for a female to ignore one of her babies, refusing to clean or mother it, but it can happen, especially if several babies are born so close together that the mother can't care for all of them at once. If a cold, neglected baby is spotted in the cage, immerse it up to the neck in very warm water and gently massage its body. Even if the baby is stiff and appears dead, try to revive it. Five minutes in warm water has turned some "dead" kits into scolding, wiggling balls of action. Once a kit is warmed by the water, wrap it in a towel and place it over a heating pad to dry. Restrain the kit under a large inverted strainer weighted down with a book or some such contraption to prevent it from wandering away. When fully recovered, it can be taken back to its mother.

POST-BIRTH CARE

If the mother and father remain in the same cage, the male will be almost as attentive to the babies as the female. However, since the mother can come into heat again within 24 hours after littering, the male should be removed within a few hours after the babies are born unless a second breeding is desired. Allowing a second breeding (breedback) is not a common practice since nursing one litter while carrying another is very taxing to the mother. It is done only when it has been extremely difficult to breed a female. If a breedback is desired, a baby creep is a must or the kits may be trampled as the breeding activity intensifies. If the male is removed to avoid a breedback, he can be returned to the cage without incident a few days later.

The parents will not object if the babies are handled, but it is best to wait until they are dried off before checking them. The kits will be fully furred and with a full set of teeth, have lots of energy, and, if the mother has done a proper cleaning job, the eyes will be open. If they are not, gently pull the lids apart or moisten a cotton-tipped swab in warm water and carefully pry the lids open.

Although chins are born with enough substance to see them through the first 12 hours without food, the first thing most of them do is claim a nipple (the mother has six) for their own. When more than one baby is born, some squabbling may take place until the new family decides who belongs where.

Should the scrapping become serious, remove the babies from the mother for a few hours. (Again, a large inverted strainer or colander weighted down with a book is an ideal place to keep them safe for a while.) Quite often the female doesn't have milk for eight hours or so, and the babies' fighting just makes the situation tense, possibly delaying the milk flow.

Since kits are born fully toothed and have a sharp set of nails, some owners clip the teeth with nail clippers and file the nails with an emery board to prevent them from biting or scratching when they nurse. This is seldom necessary and should be done only when a nursing problem develops. If the mother scolds every time the babies come near, check the female to see if her nipples are scratched and swollen. If they are sore, apply a salve to ease her discomfort and trim the kits' nails and teeth.

Sometimes nursing problems are the result of hard and swollen nipples or mastitis. Rub them with camphorated oil. The animal will look messy for a while, but the oil works like a "miracle drug" and relief and milk flow will follow shortly. Don't dust the mother until all signs of mastitis have disappeared.

The babies should be checked regularly to see if they are getting enough to eat. Undernourished kits fight and fail to put on size. Some actually seem smaller than they were at birth and constantly follow their mother, seeking milk. Well-fed babies will move around with vigor, get along with their litter mates, and start chewing on solids within two or three days after being born.

HAND-FEEDING

When the mother can't provide enough milk and the scene is one of fighting and scolding, the owner has to help feed the babies. Warm milk (whole, not skim) or a soybean milk substitute mixed 50/50 with warm water should be fed by a dropper every three or four hours for the first week and then three times a day until weaning at about six to eight weeks.

To hand-feed, take the kit from the cage and hold the animal in an upright position or have it stand. Put a drop of warm milk on its bottom lip. Hopefully it will lick it off and "chew" it—baby chins "chew" their milk—down. More often than not, it will take a lot of patience to get the baby to start eating from a dropper, but the kit will eventually figure out what you are doing. Because they are by nature used to eating often, even a few drops for the first feeding or two is a lot. Each feeding will get easier, and within days the animal will develop a real liking for its dropper-fed food.

No matter how frustrating the initial feedings may be, milk should never be forced into the baby's mouth. It will go right into the lungs and the baby will die. The kit must drink the liquid itself.

In the beginning, give the kit as much as it wants to drink; it will let you know when it is full by turning its head away and cleaning its mouth off with its tongue. When the baby starts to eat solids (a hand-fed baby seems to eat pellets later than other babies do) limit each feeding to two or three droppers full. Too much milk will prevent the animal from eating the solids it needs for proper growth.

Often the milk problem is just one of not enough, and the owner simply has to supplement. Should the kit be totally dependent on the dropper and you are not present morning, noon, and night, feed by hand whenever possible. The rest of the time provide nourishment by putting a little fresh milk into a clean bottle and hang it on the side of the cage when you leave. A daily supplement of powdered milk and oatmeal (50/50) is highly recommended for hand-fed babies.

WEANING

Usually mothers begin the weaning process when the kits are about six weeks old. By that time the babies should be eating solids and drinking plenty of water. Some ranchers wean babies at the earliest possible time, four or five weeks old, hoping to get two litters a year from each female. However, where production isn't paramount there is no harm in leaving the babies with the mother for as long as eight weeks. Actually, if the babies are quite small an extra two weeks of mother's milk may be quite beneficial even if her milk flow has decreased to some degree.

When weaned and taken from their mother, litter mates can be housed together. In fact, keeping them together seems to ease the stress weaning sometimes causes.

Check the mother for the first day or two after weaning has taken place, and if she still has milk, take the kits back for one or two feedings.

Weaners need to be watched and fed carefully. They have a tendency to over-eat or eat only what they like best, treats and supplements. Check droppings regularly and modify the kits' diet if either diarrhea or constipation occurs. Most of them settle down to an adult diet within a week or two without problems.

Because chins may need special care after weaning, babies should not be given or sold to new owners until they have been away from their mother for at least one week, preferably two, and are eating well.

Before allowing another breeding, examine the female to make sure she is, as ranchers say, "in good flesh" and eating well. Some ranchers give their breeding females a month's rest after weaning before allowing another mating. Sometimes the mother seems to make the decision to take a vacation all by herself. A female chin when extremely tired, ill, or run down simply stops coming into heat and will not breed. It's nature's way of protecting the mother and giving the potential offspring a good chance at survival.

MATING PROBLEMS

Sometimes a female just doesn't conceive—period. The male or female may be sterile or there may be another factor present that prevents conception. Unless an owner can determine which mate is sterile (and thus replace the non-parent) nothing can be done to correct the situation. On a ranch there are other animals to mate each one to, and it doesn't take long to determine which can't produce progeny. For a pet owner the situation is quite different. If kits are desired, a new animal—or even animals—will have to be purchased to produce offspring.

Before buying new breeders, make sure there aren't other factors present, factors that can be corrected.

First of all, give the pair plenty of time to reproduce. As previously noted, chins will not mate until they feel secure, and it may take months for them to feel that way.

Secondly, just because you haven't seen breeding attempts doesn't mean a mating hasn't taken place. While the majority of breedings are obvious to the owner, there's such a thing as a reserved pair, a couple that's so quiet and discreet a mating takes place without the owner seeing the usual signs. Eventually the pregnancy becomes obvious, and while one can't count off 111 days for the litter's arrival, the owner at least knows kits are on the way.

Thirdly, the female may have an infection of the uterus, vagina, or ovaries that would prevent conception. Although a brownish discharge is usually present if the animal has an infection, it doesn't always occur and sometimes the animal cleans herself so often the discharge simply isn't visible. Therefore, an infection can go unnoticed for a long time. Check the female for infection by gently inserting a cotton-tipped swab coated with Panalog® into the vagina. If all is well, when the swab is pulled out it will be coated with a clear substance. A brown or reddish stain on the swab means an infection. A veterinarian can confirm your observations and recommend medication to correct the situation. If the condition is not serious (a chronic infection may cause or may have already caused sterility), the animal should eventually be able to conceive.

A fourth factor to consider is the animal's general health. Neither overweight nor underweight animals conceive easily. Modify the animal's diet if either condition is obvious: *NO* treats or supplements for a heavy female, and lots of pellets and a regular supplement for the thin chin.

A fifth and final factor to consider is the female's heat cycle. Regular? Irregular? Nonexistent? If you've seen regular breeding attempts about once a month and conception hasn't occurred, an irregular cycle isn't a factor. But if the animals have been together for a long time, six months or more, and to the best of your knowledge no attempts have been made, you might consider having a veterinarian examine her. The vet can administer an injection (chorionic gonadotropin is one medication currently in use) to induce a heat cycle that should lead to conception.

It may take lots of time, patience, and even medical assistance to help the would-be-mother produce kits, but the results, sassy bundles of fur, can be worth the extra effort.

Ranching

Raising a herd of chinchillas for breeding and pelting purposes is different from raising pet chins in a number of ways.

First of all, the guidelines for choosing breeders are different. While health and temperament are significant, fur characteristics are of equal importance. Breeders must be bright and clear, preferably dark, and have lots of fur. The fur characteristics must complement what the rancher already has in the herd. Few, for example, would buy a long-haired light male to breed with short-haired extra-dark females no matter how beautiful the male is (yes, males are beautiful in the chin world).

To avoid mistakes, ranchers often take one or two of their own animals along when they go shopping for new stock so they can look at old and potentially new breeders side by side.

Even though ranchers can make educated guesses at how new breeders might complement their herds, there is no guarantee the lines will "nick"; that is, only the best genes will be passed along and the offspring will represent the best of their parents.

RANCH HOUSING

Ranchers also house their animals differently. While many keep their herds in basements where temperatures are relatively consistent all year long, others construct separate buildings. Such buildings must be heated or air conditioned to maintain ideal temperatures and are very expensive to operate.

Inside the unit, whether in the basement or a separate building, breeders are housed in runs, cages joined together horizontally with a long "hallway" structure that allows a male access to several females at a time.

Some ranchers have experimented with the colony system of housing where one male and a number of females are put together in a huge pen (lots of hideaways, flattened juice cans, or large creeps are provided for safety when the animals can't get along), but they are definitely in the minority.

Breeders are almost always kept separate from weaners and young adults. The breeding room is usually kept warmer for the sake of newborns, and the other area is kept cooler to promote fur growth.

Record keeping—filling in the herd book and writing out cards—is a major chore for ranchers. Herd books contain lots of vital information, including a list of all animals born on the ranch. When an animal is born, it is assigned a letter and ranch number. Each year is represented by a letter in the alphabet. 1985's letter is "P" for example, and letters rotate in alphabetical order except for G, I, O, Q, U, W, and Y, which might be confused with other letters or numbers. The first animal born in the year receives the year's letter and number 1 plus the ranch's brand for its ranch number. Those that follow receive numbers in rotation (example: BRAND-P1, BRAND-P2, etc.). Besides a letter and number, the owner enters the parents' numbers, the number of babies born in the litter, the animal's sex, its color (standard, beige, white), and any special comments the rancher feels need to be recorded.

Then a card is filled out for the animal. It lists the same information the herd book does, but also has room for show, breeding (if the animal becomes a breeder), and health records. On a large ranch the animal's location, row and cage, might also be listed.

Finally, a pen tag is put on the animal's cage; it will follow the animal as long as it is on the ranch.

Pet owners don't have to evaluate their animals often; ranchers do. Ranchers place their animals under special lights to evaluate color, fur texture, and fur quality often. They have to learn to judge quality and to replace old breeders with new when better animals appear in the herd. Only the best should be used, and good ranchers are always trying to upgrade their herds.

If your interest turns to raising a herd rather than a pet or two, there are several ways to get started, the old and the new.

STARTING A RANCH

In the past, most ranchers got started by promoters who moved throughout the United States selling breeding stock at high prices, promising to buy back offspring. Many of the companies went "bankrupt" before any buy-back occurred. While there were promoters who sold good breeding stock and bought back the animals as promised, the majority didn't. This gave the chinchilla industry a bad image. It did provide some interesting tales, though.

Promoters are still selling breeding stock. While it is one way of getting a herd without doing much legwork, you may end up paying lots of money for poor animals.

The second way to get into chins is to find a good rancher, one who will sell good stock at a reasonable price. If you're really lucky, you'll find one who will select a breeding male and top females for your herd the same way he or she would pick animals for his or her own ranch. The 1985 national grand show winner came out of such an arrangement. The problem is that it will take work, travel, and lots of patience.

Start by attending a show. If you can find a claiming day where animals are for sale and their price is listed on the cage, so much the better. It will give you an idea of both quality and pricing.

If shows are out of the question, try to locate ranchers near you and visit their units. After you've looked at many animals, you'll begin to pick out the best from the worst.

Many of today's ranchers started with poor quality and have spent years upgrading their herds. You can avoid some of the pitfalls of the past, and those ranchers who have had to work hard to breed quality into their herds can help you. Give them the chance to do it.

Showing Chinchillas

Most chinchilla shows, whether held by local, state, or national organizations, are open to the public. They offer anyone interested in chins both a chance to view some of the best of the breed and an opportunity to talk to some "chin-wise" ranchers.

At some shows competition is limited to members of a particular organization; at others, anyone can enter. This is not a place, though, for pet owners to try to compete with ranchers who have hundreds of animals to choose from for show material and whose best are truly outstanding.

Chin competition may seem a little confusing at first if you're not acquainted with the showing system, but once you familiarize yourself with the procedure—and it varies little from show to show—it's easy to understand how a grand show champion is selected.

Several hours before the actual judging starts, owners begin to arrive with their animals. When a rancher enters his or her animals, he or she is given a show cage, a cage number, a pen tag for each animal (1 to 20 standards, 1 to 20 mutations), and a registration form where all animals being entered must be listed. The rancher is expected to complete a pen tag for each animal, recording its birth date, ranch number, sex, and show (cage) number. The tag is signed and folded in such a way that the owner's name is not visible and is hung on one end of the cage that the judge or judges will see. The animal's cage number is hung on the other end of the cage for the audience to see. Finally, the corresponding animal, after a complete grooming, is caged. Owners are also required to mark each animal if they haven't done so before coming to the show. A brand and ranch number are written in the animal's ear with a felt-tip pen.

MUTATION SHOWS

When all of the animals are ready, classification for the mutation show (usually "mutes" are handled first) begins. Mutations are brought to the judging table by color groups or sections—all of the white animals, then all of the beiges, and so forth. Each section is broken down into smaller units or phases by color classifiers who hold each animal next to guide animals to determine if the animal in question is a light, medium, or a dark in its color section. (Whites are divided into groups by the presence—if any—of gray hairs mixed with the white or the presence of gray spots on the animal.) Classifiers mark the pen tags accordingly and give the cage to an animal carrier who then takes it to a records table where a show secretary records the animal's color section and phase.

The secretary also records the animal's class, which is determined by age and sex: old females, seven months or more, Class 4; old males, Class 3; young females, Class 2; young males, Class 1.

Standards are then classified using shading such as light, medium, or dark to create color phases.

When all of the animals have been classified, the record sheets are usually duplicated and distributed to the audience or posted so that everyone knows which group an animal will appear in.

Animals are divided into the various groups for the simple reason that different groups are judged by slightly different guidelines and the typical characteristics of each type of mutation or color phase are taken into consideration. For example, fur volume and clarity of color vary greatly among mutation sections. Whites tend to have lots of fur but often lack clarity of color, being creamy rather than bright white. Sapphires, on the other hand, tend to be clear and bright in color, but lack fur volume. A sapphire, by its very nature, can't be expected to be as large or as heavily furred as a white, and if only one size were acceptable for first place in all color sections, few sapphires would win a blue ribbon. But if clarity of color had to be as bright as it generally is in sapphires, few whites could claim a first place. The same is true for standards. Light standards are generally large, blocky animals, but often lack the silky fur of the darks. Few young animals, mutation or standard, could compete with adults in size or fur volume.

Furthermore, since males may be mated to seven, eight, or more females on a ranch, thus spreading their genes throughout a herd quickly, they are judged more rigorously than females.

The people evaluating chins are well-known, experienced ranchers who know the strengths and weaknesses of each group and evaluate accordingly. Many of the decision makers have received special training at seminars and have served as trainees at several shows before they have earned the title "judge."

Most shows today are multiple ribbon shows, and any number of animals meeting the specific criteria for a first place will win a blue ribbon. First-place animals must have good size and conformation for their group (*brevicaudata*-type builds are highly desirable), good color (no yellow, orange, or reddish tints or casts regardless of what color section an animal is in), and fur that stands up straight and snaps back into place when someone blows into it or the animal rolls around in the cage. Finally, a first-place animal has eye appeal. Its fur shines and has a "come hither" appearance. It has the kind of fur you just want to touch.

The judging begins with a few general announcements and the presentation of the first class of animals. The lightest animals are judged first not only in each color section but also among the color sections. Therefore, white animals are judged before whites with dark guard hair. Whites are followed by silvers, beiges, charcoals, and then blacks. In the standard show, lights are first, extra darks last.

Regardless of color phase, the animals are brought to the table in the same order: Class 4, Class 3, Class 2, and Class 1.

Once the animals are evaluated and the pen tags are marked to indicate the animal's position, judges comment on the animals and explain why they awarded the ribbons the way they did. Then pen tags are opened and the owners' names are read off for all of the animals that placed except the best two in the class, which are labeled 1A and 1B.

When all of the classes in a color section have been judged, the best old and young females (1A's from light, medium, and dark color phases) compete for female color section champion. When the winner is selected, its backup (1B) is brought to the table to compete with the rest of the 1A's.

A male color section champion and reserve are chosen next.

This procedure continues until all animals in the show have been judged.

Next, all color section champions are brought to the judging table—females in one group, males in another—and a champion male of the show and a champion female of the show are chosen. Reserves are selected from the champions' backups and the rest of the animals in each group.

Finally, the champion male and female compete to see which will win the grand show trophy. The winner's backup, either the reserve champion male or female, is brought to the table after the winner is announced and a reserve grand show champion is selected from the two animals.

After the pen tags of all of the winners have been torn open and the owners' names have been announced, the audience is invited to come to the show table to see the best of the lot.

Meanwhile, show secretaries total points on owner registration forms. Points are awarded for each position, 2 for a fifth place and 12 for a grand show champion, for example. When all of the numbers are finally added up, breeder's awards are announced.

Many ranchers consider the first place breeder's award as important as winning the trophy for a grand show champion since, especially in a highly competitive show, it takes consistency, 20 really good animals, to win the top award. Even one or two third- or fourth-place animals can cost a rancher the first-place breeder's award.

When the congratulations are over, the table is cleared and the standard show begins.

STANDARD SHOWS

The major difference in procedure between a standard show and a mutation show is that in standard competition color champions are selected from each color phase. For instance, there will be male and female color champions from the light standards, the mediums, and the darks, in contrast to the mutations that had color champions chosen from a whole section (like all the beiges, all the whites, etc.).

Shows are important to ranchers because they allow them to compare their animals with some of the best, giving them a chance to see what characteristics they should work on to improve their herds. It's also a chance to buy animals that have been evaluated by an impartial judge should a rancher not quite trust his or her own eye for quality.

Shows provide an opportunity to register animals. A registry program was started a number of years ago whereby any animal receiving a first place at a show that was judged by certified personnel could be registered with the national organization. Since 1981, the program has progressed to its second stage where only animals receiving first place at a show and having proof of a registered parent can obtain papers. The program's goals are to encourage ranchers to raise good animals and to give those ranchers written proof of their animals' quality. Registration papers also help buyers identify good bloodlines.

Besides being helpful to ranchers, shows offer spectators an opportunity to learn more about chins. So, if the chance to attend a show comes your way, by all means go, but follow a few simple rules when you attend one.

Before the show:

DON'T move any animals. If you want to look at an animal more closely or take it to the judge's table to view it under the lights, wait until the end of the show and find the owner and ask him or her to take the animal to the table for you. Chins are under stress at shows and the less they are moved or placed under hot, bright show lights, the easier it will be on the animals. Furthermore, owners have spent considerable time grooming each animal to perfection. The less the animal is moved, shaken in the cage or blown into, the better it will show. Besides, animal carriers are trying to get the animals organized for the show. When an animal is out of place, life can get hectic for show personnel.

DON'T carry any liquid (coffee and soda are usually available at shows) above the animals. Coffee has been accidentally spilled on animals before a show with devastating effects on the chin's fur.

DON'T make sudden movements or loud noises around the animals.

DON'T try to carry on a conversation with a rancher when he or she is combing animals or trying to fill out pen cards and registration forms accurately. Most ranchers love to talk about the animals and will gladly answer any questions you have, but wait until they've finished their entry forms and are enjoying a cup of coffee. Then, **DO** query away.

DON'T smoke near the animals. (Many show chairpersons request that you not smoke in the show area, period, so check the local rules before lighting up.)

DO walk around and look at the animals, especially the many kinds of mutations. By comparing and contrasting many animals, you can learn to pick out quality. Besides, they're fun just to look at.

During the show:

DO pick up classification sheets. They will help you follow the show's progress and give you a place to record notes on if you wish.

DO ask questions if you become confused.

DON'T go near the judging table. Besides blocking the audience's view for a minute or two, any brightly colored clothing reflects on the animals, making it more difficult for a judge to determine clarity of color on a chin.

DO stay around for the finals, when the very best animals are placed on the table, especially if you think you might want to become a rancher. Viewing the winners and listening to judges' and ranchers' comments regarding those animals is one of the best ways to learn about quality in chinchillas.

National Chinchilla Shows

Many chins had been shown competitively at informal field days and regional shows by the early 1950's. The demand for a national show was a logical outgrowth of the early shows, and in 1954 the Minnesota branch of the national organization hosted the first such show in Minneapolis. One of Floyd Hayes's chins won the first national grand show trophy ever presented, and an animal from the Cambridge Grant Chinchilla Farm took the reserve position.

The following year the national was held in Omaha, Nebraska, and, in addition to the grand and reserve grand show trophies, breeder's awards at the national level were started. S. W. Pangborn won the first-place breeder's award that year and in 1956 as well.

Mutations didn't compete at a national show until 1965. The first grand show trophy went to the Somovia Chin Ranch and the reserve to C. George Delaney, a man who had worked closely with Nick Tower and the Crown of Sunset beiges.

Several ranchers' names have appeared often in the national winner's column. Iowan Harold Anderson holds the record for winning the most standard grand show championships to date—six of them. In 1959, 1960, and 1971 he won both grand show and reserve grand show. He also won the first-place breeder's award six times.

In mutations, Robert Gunning (Gunning blacks) won three grand shows and four reserves. From 1977 to 1980, Enchanted Farms of California dominated mutations, winning grand show four years in a row.

The location of the national show varies, and in the early years it was situated wherever it was easily accessible to the majority of ranchers. Since then, the national organization, Empress, which divided the United States into four regions with the lines of demarcation running north to south (the West Coast is in Region 1, the East Coast is in Region 4), has decided to rotate the show's location so that all ranchers have a national near them once every four years.

Before members can enter animals at the national, they must qualify at a sanctioned state show, one organized by Empress members and judged by certified personnel. A rancher is entitled to enter as many animals at the national (up to 20 standards, 20 mutations) as ribbons have been won. In other words, if a rancher wins 20 ribbons at a state show, he can enter 20 animals at the national.

Besides the usual awards, there are several traveling trophies given each year in memory of chinchilla pioneers. Among them is the M. E. Caraway trophy, which recognizes "Doc" Caraway's work with mutations. The Caraway trophy is awarded to the winner of the first-place breeder's award in mutations. The Mathias F. Chapman trophy, which recognizes Chapman's struggle and success in establishing chins in America, goes to the winner of the first-place breeder's award in standards.

Attending a national show gives one a chance to see some of the best animals in the country. It is an opportunity few serious chinchilla ranchers ignore.

Sources of Information

The most convenient source of information and supplies is a local pet store, but sometime you may want more information than the shopkeeper can give. Maybe you'd like to meet and talk to other chinchilla owners or attend a show to see what other chins look like. Or perhaps your interest in the animals has changed, like Chapman's did, from owning one to raising many.

The following directory is a beginning list of places where one can find chinchilla information.

Chinchatter
6420 E. Florence Avenue
Bell Gardens, California 90201

. . . is the official monthly newsletter of the Southwest Chinchilla Group, Inc., and has been published since 1952. Its content is aimed more at a rancher than a pet owner (unless you're breeding animals) but does contain lots of practical information regarding diet, disease, and care of young animals that you may find interesting. *Chinchatter* publishes a list of shows where visitors are welcome to attend. For subscription information send them a stamped self-addressed envelope (SASE).

Empress Chinchilla Breeders Cooperative, Inc.
P.O. Box 402
Morrison, Colorado 80465

. . . is the national organization for chinchilla ranchers. While membership is limited to breeders, the organization does sell the *Rancher's Handbook* to non-members. The *Handbook* was recently updated and is now available in looseleaf form so new sections can be added easily. The handbook specializes in ranching techniques and is especially strong in the area of chinchilla reproduction. Meant for the serious and dedicated chin owner, it's available from the national office (send a SASE for information).

Empress members sponsor a number of state shows and field days throughout the United States and a national show each March. Visitors are welcome, and attending such a show is a good way to learn a lot about chins from some of the old-timers who have worked with the animals for years. It's also a chance to see some of the country's best chins—real "eye-poppers." Contact the secretary of the organization for the time and place of a show near you.

Kline Chinchilla Research Foundation
P.O. Box 451
Utica, Illinois 61373

. . . offers a publication full of information about chinchilla husbandry (send a SASE for price). Although prepared with ranchers in mind, it contains lots of ideas pet owners could use.

National Chinchilla Breeders of Canada
R.R. 10
Brampton
Ontario, Canada L6V 3N2

. . . publishes a monthly newsletter (write for current price). If you live in Canada, you may want to contact NCBC for names of ranchers near you or shows in your area.

Princeton Process
501 S. Main Street
Spring City, Pennsylvania 19475

. . . is a pelt processing/marketing outlet that is currently expanding to offer other services. It now publishes a monthly newsletter that lists chin shows (particularly in the East). The newsletter's staff may be able to help you locate local ranchers and shows (remember that SASE).

Bibliography

"The Andersons," *Empress Chinchilla Magazine*, May, 1967.

"Care for the New Arrival," *International Chinchilla Ranch Advisor*, June, 1968.

"Chinchilla Digest," Koch Laboratory (publisher), 1971 and 1972 editions.

Dewenter, Robert, "Chinchillas Go to School," *Empress Chinchilla Magazine*, 1968.

"Empress Registry," *Empress Chinchilla Breeder*, December, 1981.

"Feeding the Chinchilla," *Chinchatter*, October, 1971.

Greenfield, Bob, *Richardson Daily News* (Texas), January 16, 1976.

Gunning, Bob, "Development of Black Velvet," *Empress Chinchilla Magazine*, January, 1969.

Hanney, Peter, *Rodents*, Taplinger (publisher), 1975.

Hemmingsen, A. B., *Principles of Chinchilla Ranching*, Division West Chinchilla Corporation (publisher), Omaha, Nebraska, 1968.

Herdman, Glendon R., "Chinchillas," *The Farm Quarterly*, Autumn, 1949.

Hunt, Hollis, "Droppings," *Empress Chinchilla Breeder*, April, 1973.

Keagy, Richard (D. V. M.), "Diseases of the Chinchilla," *Chinchatter*, November, 1972.

Kelley, Dr. E. T., edited by Dr. J. L. Gallentine, *A Textbook of Chinchilla Genetics*, (self-published), 1970.

Kline, Alice, "The Use of Solid Bottom Cages," *Empress Chinchilla Breeder*, November, 1972.

Koch, Bernard (D. V. M.), "Chatty Chin," (health problems in chins column), *Chinchilla Reporter*, May, 1970.

Koch, Bernard (D. V. M.), "Chronic Chinchilla Fungus," *Empress Chinchilla Breeder*, May, 1979.

Lien, Merle T., "Guide Lines for the New Rancher," Parts 1 and 2, *Empress Chinchilla Magazine*, January and February, 1968.

"National Show Results," *Empress Chinchilla Breeder*, June, 1985.

"Pages of History," *Chinchilla International*, May, 1968.

Rancher's Handbook, Empress Chinchilla Breeder's Co-operative, Inc., (publisher), 1970.

"Rodents Worth Their Weight in Gold," *Popular Mechanics*, December, 1937.

Sulivan, Loyd, "The Violet Mutation," *Empress Chinchilla Breeder*, May, 1985.

Sweeny, Sebert, "Chinchilla Reflections—Part 1," *Empress Chinchilla Magazine*, February, 1968.

"The Habitat of the Wild Chinchilla," Parts 1 and 2, *Empress Chinchilla Breeder*, November and December, 1978. (Reprinted from *National Chinchilla Breeders of Canada Bulletin*, Vol. 32, No. 12, March, 1978.)

"Then and Now . . . The Chapman Story," *Chinchilla Reporter*, July, 1969.

Tower, Nick, "Crown of Sunset Story," *International Chinchilla Ranch Advisor*, June, 1968.

Von Blon, John L. "Naturalizing the Chinchilla," *Scientific American*, December, 1925.

Index